STARTING A NEW LIFE IN ITALY

The Ultimate Relocating Guide for Nomads

ALPHONSINE PELLETIER

©Copyrights, Alphonsine Pelletier, 2024 – All rights reserved.

The content of this book may not be reproduced, duplicated, or transmitted without direct permission from the author or publisher.

Under no circumstances will any blame or legal responsibility be held against the publisher or author for any damages, reparation, or monetary loss due to the information contained within this book, either directly or indirectly. You recognize that you are responsible for your own choices, actions, and results.

Legal Notice: This book is copyright-protected. This book is only for personal use. You cannot amend, distribute, sell, use, quote, or paraphrase any part or the content within this book without the author's or publisher's consent.

Disclaimer Notice: Even though all efforts have been made to present the most up-to-date, complete, and reliable information, this book may not constitute the most up-to-date legal information and does not and is not intended to replace the advice of a legal expert. The content of this book has been derived from various sources. Readers acknowledge that the author is not engaging in rendering any legal, medical, financial, or professional advice. Instead, this book's information, content, and materials are for general information purposes only.

By reading this document, the reader agrees that under no circumstances is the author responsible for any losses, direct or indirect, sustained as the result of the use of the information contained within this document, including but not limited to errors, omissions, or inaccuracies.

Luggage with Italy's Flag Colors

Through her books, Alphonsine Pelletier delves into the practicalities of relocating to a new country. Her writing is marked by a deep sense of empathy, offering readers valuable insights, tips, and practical advice for navigating the intricacies of relocation. She combines her personal stories with well-researched information, ensuring that her readers are well-prepared for the challenges and delights of a new territory. The author understands that the decision to move abroad is both exhilarating and intimidating, something she experienced when she relocated from Paris to Los Angeles. Her books aim to be a trusted companion for anyone who finds themselves at the crossroads of a significant life change. With the right mindset and her guidance, readers can transform the uncertainties of relocation into a life-enriching experience and discover a sense of home in even the farthest corners of the world.

So, whether you are looking to relocate or for new places to explore, you will find that her travel books are more than guides; they are a vision of everyday life in a new country. Italy is where you want to be if you want to enjoy year-round sunny weather, be surrounded by spectacular views, and indulge in incredible food while affording the living costs. The author invites you to turn the page and immerse yourself in what could be your new life. Discover all you need to know about the country, the customs, the bureaucracy, and the locals. Learn about the different visas and pick up a few Italian expressions. With "Starting a New Life in Italy: The Ultimate Relocating Guide for Nomads," your adventure begins now. Don't wait; turn the page and start living your dream.

Contents

GETTING TO KNOW ITALY | CONOSCERE L'ITALIA....3

ETIQUETTE RULES AND LOCAL CUSTOMS | REGOLE DEL GALATEO E USANZE LOCALI 9

THINGS PEOPLE COMPLAIN THE MOST ABOUT ITALY | LE COSE DI CUI CI SI LAMENTA DI PIÙ IN ITALIA 15

    Funny Quotes About Italy | Citazioni Divertenti Sull'italia 19

LANGUAGE | LINGUA 21

    Dating In Italian | Appuntamenti In Italiano 26

    Common Expressions In Italian: | Espressioni Comuni In Italiano 29

    Common Vocabulary Words In Italian: | Parole Comuni Del Lessico Italiano 31

    Common Slang Expressions In Italian: | Espressioni Gergali Comuni 32

    Common Verbs In Italian | Verbi Comuni In Italiano 33

MOVING TO ITALY | TRASFERIRSI IN ITALIA 37

    Take A Moment 37

    General Rules | Regole Generali 38

    Shipping Your Car To Italy | Spedire La Vostra Auto 41

    International Moving And Shipping Companies | Società Di Traslochi E Spedizioni Internazionali 43

    Moving With Children In Italy | Trasferirsi In Italia Con I Bambini 44

    Moving With Animals | Trasferirsi Con Animali 45

    Pros Of Living In Italy | Vantaggi Della Vita In Italia 48

    Cons Of Living In Italy | Aspetti Negativi Della Vita In Italia 49

ITALIAN ENTRY REQUIREMENTS | REQUISITI D'INGRESSO ITALIANI 51

Etias | European Travel Information And Authorization System . 51

Schengen Area / Zone | Zona Schengen 53

Paperwork | Carta 56

Visa-Free Entry | Ingresso Senza Visto 58

Airport Transit Visa / Type A Visa | Visto Di Transito Aeroportuale (Tipo A) 59

Italy Temporary Visas | Visti Per Soggiorno Temporaneo 60

Schengen Visas (Usv) / Type C Visas | Visti Schengen 61

Schengen Visa With Limited Territorial Validity (Ltv) | Visto Con Validità Territoriale Limitata 64

Seasonal Work Visa | Visto Di Lavoro Stagionale 65

Family Reunification Visa | Visto De Ricongiungimento Familiare 65

Long-Stay Or "National" Visa (Nv) / Type D Visas | Visto Per Soggiorni Di Lunga Durata O "Visto Nazionale" 66

THE NOMAD LIFE | LA VITA DA NOMADE 71

Why Choose The Nomad Life | Perchè Scegliere La Vita Da Nomade 72

What Are The Cons Of A Nomad Life | Quali Sono I Contro Di Una Vita Da Nomade 72

Few Ways To Make A Living As A Nomad In Italy | Alcuni Modi Per Guadagnarsi Da Vivere Come Nomade 73

The Digital Nomads | I Nomadi Digitali 74

Best Jobs For Digital Nomads | Lavori Migliori Per Nomadi Digitali 75

Where To Stay As A Digital Nomad In Italy | Alloggi Per Nomani Digitali In Italia 76

NOMADS VISAS | VISTI PER NOMADI DIGITALI 81

Self-Employment Visas | Visto Per Lavoro Autonomo 83

Italy Investor Visa | Visto Per Investitori 89

Differences Between Italy Self-Employed And Investor Visas: 93

Italy Digital Nomad Visa | Visto Per Nomadi Digitali In Italia 94

WORKING IN ITALY | LAVORARE IN ITALIA 99

Italy Work Visa | Visto Per Lavoro In Italia 101

How To Start A Business In Italy | Come Avviare Un'attività In Italia 104

Hiring A Staff In Italy | Assumere Personale In Italia 107

Renting A Space For Your Business In Italy | Affittare Uno Spazio Per La Vostra Attività In Italia 109

Registering A Foreign Company In Italy | Registrazione Di Una Società Straniera In Italia 109

Italy Start-Up Visa (Isv) | Visto Lavoro Autonomo Start Up 110

Registering Your Brand In Italy | Registrazione Del Marchio In Italia 114

STUDYING IN ITALY | STUDIARE IN ITALIA 119

Italian Education System | Sistema Educativo Italiano 121

Homeschool In Italy | Educazione Domestica/ Istruzione Parentale 123

Universities In Italy | Università In Italia 124

Top Italian Universities 126

Italy Student Visa | Visto Studenti 127

Pros Of Studying In Italy | Vantaggi Dello Studiare 129

Cons Of Studying In Italy | Svantaggi Dello Studiare 130

RETIRING IN ITALY | PENSIONE IN ITALIA 133

Why Retire In Italy | Perchè Andare In Pensione In Italia 135

"Cons" Of Retiring In Italy | Svantaggi Del Pensionamento In Italia 136

Italy Elective Residency Visa (Type D Visa) | Visto Residenza Elettiva 136

What You Need For An Italian Elective Residence Visa: 139

BUREAUCRACY IN ITALY | BUROCRAZIA IN ITALIA 143

- What You Need To Get A Spid: 144
- Integration Agreement | Accordo Di Integrazione 144
- Register Of Vital Statistics | Anagrafe 145
- Police Headquarters / Police Central Office / Main Police Station | Questura 145
- Immigration Office | Sportello Unico Per L'immigrazione 146
- Certificate Of No Impediment 147
- Syndicates/Associations/ Non-Profits | Patronati 150
- Italy Residence Permit | Permesso Di Soggiorno 151
- What You Need For Italy Residence Permit: 153
- Tax Assistant Center | Centro Di Assistenza Fiscale (Caf) 154
- Taxes In Italy | Tasse In Italia 155
- Individual Tax Identification Number/Tax Code | Codice Fiscale 157
- Self-Employed Tax Code / Number | Partita Iva: Partita Individuale Di Identificazione Fiscale 159
- Currency In Italy | Valuta In Italia 160
- Banking In Italy | Banche In Italia 162
- Money Transfer | Bonifico Bancario 163

HEALTHCARE IN ITALY | SANITÀ IN ITALIA 167

- What You Need To Register For Italy Health Coverage: 169
- Italy Emergency Phone Numbers: 170
- Pharmacies In Italy | Farmacie 171
- Alternative Therapies In Italy | Terapie Alternative 172
- Mental Healthcare | Assistenza Sanitaria Per La Salute Mentale 173
- Mental Healthcare For Children | Assistenza Sanitaria Per La Salute Mentale Dei Bambini 174

LIFE IN ITALY | LA VITA IN ITALIA ... 177

- Weather | Meteo ... 177
- Costs Of Living In Italy | Costo Della Vita In Italia ... 178
- Consumer Goods In Italy | Beni Di Consumo In Italia ... 180
- Utilities In Italy | Servizi Pubblici In Italia ... 180
- Getting Around In Italy | Muoversi In Italia ... 187
- Buying A Car In Italy | Comprare Un'auto ... 188
- Transportation In Italy | Trasporti ... 190
- Real Estate In Italy | Immobiliare In Italia ... 192
- Buying Property In Italy | Acquistare Una Proprietà / Comprare Un Immobile ... 194
- Landlords | Locatori/Terreni ... 196
- Tenants/Renters | Inquilini/Locatari ... 196

CITIZENSHIP IN ITALY | CITTADINANZA IN ITALIA ... 201

- What You Need To Apply For Citizenship In Italy: ... 201
- Italian Citizenship Through Marriage | Cittadinanza Per Matrimonio ... 203
- Italian Citizenship Through Residency Or Naturalization | Cittadinanza Per Residenza ... 204
- Citizenship Based On Ancestry Or By Descent | Cittadinanza Basata Su Un'ascendenza ... 205
- Dual Citizenship | Doppia Cittadinanza / Cittadinanza Doppia 206

WHERE TO LIVE IN ITALY | DOVE VIVERE IN ITALIA ... 209

- Northern Italy | Italia Settentrionale / Nord Italia ... 210
- Central Italy | Italia Centrale ... 216
- Southern Italy | Mezzogiorno / Italia Meridionale ... 221

TEST YOUR KNOWLEDGE | TESTA LA TUA CONOSCENZA ... 231

ANSWERS | RISPOSTE ... 233

VOCABULARY / LEXIQUE | VOCABOLARIO/ LESSICO....... 239

REFERENCES | BIBLIOGRAPHIA... 243

Italy, Europe

GETTING TO KNOW ITALY
CONOSCERE L'ITALIA

Whether you are attracted by the culture or the people, the reasons why someone would want to live in one of the most beautiful European countries and the fifth most visited country in the world are endless. Actually, only some countries can compete with Italy regarding history, architecture, music, literature, art, and food. Located in the South of Europe, bordering France, Austria, and Slovenia, this boot-shaped peninsula, known for its Mediterranean climate, has quite a diverse topography from the North to the South: beautiful beaches, breathtaking views, massive mountains, lakes, rolling hills, and mild and sunny weather. Part of the European Union, EU (a political and economic union of member states located primarily in Europe,) it is also a member of the Schengen Area (a zone comprising European countries that have abolished passport control at their mutual borders) and the Single Market (the free movement of goods, services, capital, and people within the EU). Like most EU countries, it has replaced its former currency, the Lira, with the Euro (€).

Some people might assume that it is the oldest country in Europe because they naturally associate it with the Roman Empire, even though historically, Italy was a province of the Roman Empire until 1861, when it became one country.

As a side note, Portugal is, in reality, the oldest country in Europe if you consider that it has had the same borders since 1139. So, before Italy became one country, it was made of small independent states, each with its own laws and traditions. Today, those cultural differences are found in several aspects of Italian culture due to Italy being dominated by different civilizations throughout history.

The word "Italian" refers to a person of Italian origins or nationality and the official language spoken in the country. Switzerland, San Marino, a microstate located within Italy, and Vatican City, a city-state located within Rome, the capital city of Italy, are the other places where Italian is also spoken. Some Italians in the 1900s emigrated to the USA, Brazil, and Argentina, which means it is not unusual to hear Italian spoken in those countries since some of their descendants still speak the language.

However, even though most Italians, especially the younger generation, speak English, you might encounter a language barrier if you find yourself in a small village with few foreigners. That is because, even though Italian is the official language, regions such as Sicily, Venice, and Napoli still have their own dialects that sound very different from mainstream Italian.

> **Note:** Depending on where you live, the language barrier can be the biggest obstacle to integration in Italy.

Most Italians identify as Catholic, which makes sense given that Italy is considered the birthplace of the Roman Catholic Church. Their tie to the Catholic faith is even more strengthened by the fact that the Vatican happens to be the Catholic Church's headquarters and home to the Pope. Despite that, there are quite a few disparities in how Italians practice their faith because religious traditions and practices differ from one region to the other. Besides religion, Italians still hold traditional values such as family and cultural traditions. The country still has to recognize same-sex marriage but has legalized same-sex partnerships and uses the gender-neutral pronoun "*Loro*," a literal translation of English "They."

Ask any kid who Leonardo, Michelangelo, Donatello, and Raphael are; chances are the answer will be Ninja Turtles. However, before they became Teenage Mutant Ninja Turtles, Leonardo da Vinci (artist and inventor), Michelangelo Buonarroti (sculptor, painter, and architect), Donatello di Niccolò di Betto Bardi (sculptor), and Raffaello Sanzio da Urbino (painter and architect) were famous Italian Renaissance artists whose work and ideas continue to impact our world today.

> **Note**: Leonardo di Caprio, the famous American actor, was named after Leonardo da Vinci.

Italy has a wide range of economic industries, which means the economy is strong. Italians are hard workers and take pride in their work ethics. Even if tourism is the main contributor, the agricultural (cheese, wine), manufacturing (textiles), and fashion industries make it one of Europe's most significant economic forces. The different sectors mean endless opportunities for self-employed people and those who want to start a business. Italy has many co-working spaces, and many cities have public libraries, cafes, and other areas where Wi-Fi is available, making it the perfect country for Digital Nomads.

If Armani, Prada, Gucci, or Versace ring a bell, that is because they all hail from Italy, and just in case you didn't know it yet, Italians are very fashionable. Cinephiles might be fans of Fellini and Rossellini unless, like me, you became a fan of Roberto Benigni after watching "Life is Beautiful." Opera or classical music enthusiasts would probably associate Vivaldi and Puccini with Italy. But let's not forget Pavarotti, Andrea Bocelli, Sofia Loren, and, of course, the most famous cars in the world, Ferrari, Bugatti, Lamborghini, Maserati, and to my surprise Fiat (*Fabbrica Italiana Automobili Torino*) because growing up, I thought Fiat was French and came from the Latin "fiat," meaning "Let it be done."

> **Note**: Do not mistake Donatella Versace, the famous Italian designer, for Donatello, the Renaissance artist.

If you plan to visit Italy, look for smaller local restaurants instead of following tourist guidebook recommendations. Another way to taste regional specialties is to attend a festival or celebration, "*Sagra*," which can be an excellent way to immerse yourself in the local culture. I used to like my pasta until I ate homemade pasta in Italy. Their ingredients are top quality, meaning your food will still taste amazing even if you are not a great cook. Italy offers a variety of healthy culinary options that would leave any food enthusiast craving for more. And if you are a fan of the Mediterranean diet, which is rich in fruits, vegetables, and olive oil, what better place to be? Moreover, Italy has been recognized for having relatively high life expectancies, with Sardinia being one of the "Blue Zones" in the world. That's because, besides genetics, Italy possesses all the other factors that are said to affect life expectancy: strong social connections (Italy values family ties), regular physical activity (lots of walking in Italy), healthcare (Italy has an excellent healthcare system), and good socioeconomic conditions. And, as you can guess, the country is the world's number one pasta exporter, as "the average Italian eats about 23 kilos of pasta per year," according to Assoutenti, a consumer group.

You can't write about Italy without mentioning soccer or football. The Italian national football team is one of the most successful teams in the sport's history, having won four World Cup championships, with AC Milan, Inter Milan, and Juventus being the most famous teams.

> **Note:** Italian football fanatics are called "*Tifosi*" (fans), and the game is "*Calcio*," meaning "Kick" or "Strike" in English.

Despite the fading presence of the Mafia, Italy remains a safe country to travel to and live in. "In 2021, 69.2 percent of Italian respondents declared to trust the State Police." (Statista.com) Depending on your country of origin and financial situation, you might find life more affordable and enjoyable in Italy. You will have a higher quality of life and access to a great health system, while getting the right visa will give you direct access to the Schengen area and, thus, to the rest of Europe. Even though the reasons why Italy is one of the best countries to live in are infinite, there are still a few rules that one should be aware of.

Lake Como, Italy

ETIQUETTE RULES AND LOCAL CUSTOMS

REGOLE DEL GALATEO E USANZE LOCALI

Some Italian towns are so charming that you will feel like they are straight out of a fairy tale. So, to prevent any disenchantment, below are a few rules and local customs you should be aware of when visiting or settling in Italy.

When in Italy, surrender to "*la dolce far niente,*" the sweetness in the art of doing nothing or "*l'art de ne rien faire*" as the French call it, and enjoy "*la dolce vita*"; the sweet life, often characterized by a love of good food, wine, art, and fashion.

Talking about fashion, Italian men and women have a timeless, sophisticated sense of style that exudes glamor and style. They don't dress to impress but prioritize elegance and quality over fashion trends. Women wear leggings with blazers, tunics, or cardigans that cover the back. If you like revealing clothes, crop tops, sleeveless cutouts, and backless or low-cut dresses, you would want to cover your knees and shoulders if you plan to visit religious or touristy places. Use common sense and dress according to the context because many famous Italian attractions submit visitors to a strict dress code.

> **Note to women**: Cobblestone streets date from centuries ago. It's better to wear platform shoes instead of high heels to avoid any injury.

Besides "*Ciao*" or "*Salve,*" both meaning "Hello," "*Buongiorno*" (Good morning) and "*Buonasera*" (Good evening), Italians also use a handshake or a kiss on the cheek "*un Bacio Sulla Guancia*" to greet each other. Usually, it's two kisses, one on each cheek, but sometimes you might be expected to give three kisses, depending on which part of the country you are in. Like most Europeans, Italians consider hugging far more intimate than kissing on the cheeks.

> **Note**: Always greet the owner or the salesperson whenever you enter a shop. And remember that European sizes are different for clothes or shoes, so always try before buying.

If you are a man, don't call your girlfriend "*Bambina,*" which means "baby or little girl," in public. People will find you repulsive because of the sexual connotation. Call her "*Bimba,*" short for "*Bambina*" instead. Same for women, you can call your boyfriend "*Bimbo*" but avoid "*Bambino*" (little or baby boy) when in public. Another word women should avoid calling their male partners in public is "*Papà*" unless they are talking about their "Dad."

> **Note**: While in Italy, do not mistake "*Papa*" (Pope) with "*Papà*" (Dad).

Even if "Starbucks has allegedly based its coffee shop model on Italy's cafe culture," Italian "*caffè*" (coffee) remains the best in the world, and the Italians take great pride in it. An espresso is a coffee or, more precisely, a simple shot of regular coffee, which tends to be very strong in Italy.

> **Note**: Though appreciated, tipping in restaurants will be at your discretion.

Contrary to some beliefs, Italians don't drink excessively; thus, alcoholic beverages should be enjoyed in moderation. Getting "wasted" or overly drunk is not well looked upon. But they party hard and late because Italian nightlife often starts late, with many clubs becoming livelier after midnight and staying open until early morning. Major cities like Milan, Rome, Florence, and Naples have vibrant nightlife scenes, with popular tourist destinations like Ibiza, Sardinia, and the Amalfi Coast being renowned for clubs that attract both locals and international visitors.

> **Note**: It is illegal to drink and drive in Italy.

You might think they are crazy drivers because they are high-speed drivers, but they will assure you that they are just excellent drivers who have developed powerful reflexes. So, if you must cross a street, know that drivers won't stop for you unless you are just as aggressive crossing the street as they are driving. So, never stop mid-walk or hesitate while crossing streets. But if you take public transportation, be ready to give up your seat to older people; it is the right thing to do and mostly expected. Italians have very conservative values; among them are family and respect.

Suppose the old person you give your seat to is a woman, then she should be addressed as "*Madre*" (Mother). You will address women according to their marital status. A married woman is a "*Signora*" (Mrs.), and a single woman is a "*Signorina*" (Miss). "*Cara*" (Dear) is the informal way to address any female, whether they are a close friend or a relative. If you find yourself in a situation where you have no idea how to address a woman you are not familiar with, pay attention to how the people around you are addressing her and follow their lead. A man will be addressed as "*Signore*" (Mr.)

> **Note**: You will only call someone by their first name if you are well acquainted with them or if they give you permission.

I took the train for a year in London, and I could have looked at a man right in the eyes and still not tell if he noticed. On the other side, it's quite common to smile or make eye contact with strangers in Italy; only be aware that by staring back or smiling, you might unwillingly send the message that you find them attractive.

> **Note to women**: Avoid prolonged eye contact with men if you're not interested in being approached.

It is universal knowledge that the number 13 is the number one unlucky number. Only in Italy, the number 17 (*diciassette*) is often considered unlucky due to its resemblance to the Roman numeral "XVII," which can be rearranged to form the Latin word "VIXI," which means "I have lived" or worse, "I am dead" in English. The aversion to the number 17 is so strong in Italian culture that you might notice that some buildings, hotels, or floors skip the number 17, similar to how some buildings in other cultures skip the 13th floor.

"*Corna*" is a hand gesture like the "devil horns" and is used to ward off the "evil eye" (*Malocchio*), a curse brought by envy or jealousy. Another way to keep the evil spirits away in Italy is to carry a small piece of iron. If carrying a piece of iron is too problematic, you can either touch the iron or throw some salt over your left shoulder. And for those of you dreaming of meeting that special person during your stay in Italy, if you don't want to jeopardize your luck, don't rest a hat on the bed.

Selling cannabis in Italy is considered a criminal offense that can lead to imprisonment. Only medical cannabis is authorized. However, if you are caught in possession of a very small amount for recreational use, you might get a formal warning, a fine, or it might be taken away.

> **Note**: You can get CBD or "*Cannabis Light*" in Italian, at tobacco shops (*Tabaccherie*), automated machines, or specialized chain stores and cooperatives, or have it delivered to your house.

However, like any other country, Italy also has its share of challenges and potential drawbacks, which, fortunately, remain minimal considering everything the country has to offer.

Civitanova Alta, Marche Region, Italy

THINGS PEOPLE COMPLAIN THE MOST ABOUT ITALY

LE COSE DI CUI CI SI LAMENTA DI PIÙ IN ITALIA

As I mentioned in my book "Starting a New Life in Portugal," I think of the first year of living abroad as the "honeymoon phase," where everything is new and exciting. Life usually becomes harder when reality sets in, and the feeling of vacationing fades. Anyone who lives abroad knows this feeling because that's when you start feeling nostalgic and miss home the most. So, if you can, try to return to your home country whenever you can; something to remember when you choose your visa. Having the possibility to travel outside of Italy will play a significant role in how much you enjoy the country.

Although you may not experience culture shock moving to Italy, be wary of thieves and pickpockets in busy tourist areas, expect crowded streets and increased prices in big cities like Venice, Florence, or Rome, and don't be surprised if you don't hear a lot of English since most Italians don't speak a second language, especially in small villages. Italy might have a Mediterranean climate, but the temperatures will vary depending on where you live. If you decide to live in the North of Italy, remember that winters can be harsh, with temperatures around 0°C or 32°F, which is still mild compared to Northern countries like Norway or Iceland. Nevertheless, make sure the house you are renting has a heating system installed.

We already mentioned "*La dolce far niente*," or the art of relaxing and doing nothing. You might find it fascinating, but for others, this ability to spend hours sitting in a café without doing anything "productive" can be irritating. Not to mention the art of "*Arrangiarsi*" or "we will figure it out," which can be perceived as a form of pessimism and lack of motivation by some. It's also helpful to know the local customs and schedules to plan your activities accordingly. If you need to run errands between 11:30 a.m. and 2:00 p.m., think twice because some businesses may be closed for lunch breaks (*pausa pranzo*), a customary lunchtime, or go home and take a short nap (*un riposo*), especially on hot summer days. While this may seem counterintuitive to some who prioritize business over self-care, remember that Sardinia, the second-largest Italian island in the Mediterranean Sea after Sicily, is one of the "longevity hotspots," where the inhabitants can live up to 100 years. But if you are self-employed or retired, this should not be an issue since you will set your own schedule and run your errands at your own hours.

Regrettably, Italy has a high number of fatalities resulting from road accidents due to the way they drive. I used to think, "If I can drive in Paris, I can drive anywhere." I have since changed my mind. If you can drive in Italy, you can drive anywhere. But rest assured. In 2024, for road safety reasons, Bologna became the first major city to bring in a 30km/h limit, equivalent to 18mph, according to theguardian.com. Also, Italy's public transportation is pretty good, and depending on where you live you might not necessarily need a car, which should lower stress and help reduce air pollution. And those narrow roads are just a fact for most of Europe, nothing specific to Italy.

Italians might be the "most romantic people in the world," even though the French might disagree, but like everyone else, they also have their flaws. Always be ready to change your plans because, like their trains, they are not always punctual, and customer service could be better. And they curse a lot, a trait they share with most Mediterranean countries; ask the Portuguese or French. However, remember that someone living in the North might not have the same experience as someone living in the South of Italy, as it all comes down to personal experience.

Despite past invasions, Italy is not typically considered a multicultural country in the same sense as some other nations with a long history of immigration and cultural diversity because, unlike other European countries, its colonial empire was very small and didn't last long. However, in recent decades, the country has seen increased cultural diversity due to immigration from various parts of the world. Cities like Milan, Rome, and Turin have become more cosmopolitan and multicultural, with residents and communities representing various nationalities, languages, and cultures.

Sadly, in contrast with the increase in immigration and the number of wealthy foreigners who are choosing to live or retire in Italy, many young Italians have been leaving the country due to a lack of job opportunities, a high unemployment rate, and the fact that Italy's system is not meritocratic, making it difficult to get promoted. Add to that the corruption and bribery in various sectors, either government, public services, or businesses, and you will understand why people complain about Italy.

Excessive bureaucracy and the frequent changes in government that make it difficult to implement long-term policies have frustrated people, not to mention the state of public infrastructures such as transportation and roads in some areas that might be outdated or in need of maintenance. And if you choose to live in rural areas, you might have to deal with slower and unreliable internet connections. But like anywhere else, your experience of Italy will depend on your financial means, who you surround yourself with, and where you choose to live.

I find the exuberance of Italians to be contagious. They are enthusiastic, pleasant, and good-natured people who are always willing to lend a hand, even though, at times, they will also give their opinion even when not asked about it. However, making new friends and adjusting to a new country takes time, no matter where you go, and Italy is no exception. You will need to adjust your expectations and be open to whatever turns life takes, hoping it won't take too long before you can share a cappuccino or sip wine at sunset with a new friend.

Most importantly, remember that when living in Italy, you become Italian! Meaning that after a while, what looks like obstacles will become routine and part of life. But if you still see these "cons" as problems, you might not be ready to move to Italy because integration might be challenging. Otherwise, keep reading!

FUNNY QUOTES ABOUT ITALY

Citazioni Divertenti Sull'italia

- ☞ *"Everything you see I owe to spaghetti."* Sophia Loren, Italian actress, while talking about her curvy body and paying homage to Italian food

- ☞ *"In Italy, we have a saying: The appetite comes with eating."* In other words, the more you eat, the hungrier you get. Silvio Berlusconi, former Italian Prime Minister, in an interview with David Frost, "Frost Over the World" (2008)

- ☞ *"Life is a combination of magic and pasta."* Federico Fellini, movie director, interview with Dick Cavett, "The Dick Cavett Show" (1971)

- ☞ *"Italians can do everything, but they can't do punctuality."* a popular Italian saying by Giuseppe Garibaldi, a former Italian deputy

- ☞ *"I don't like to drive. I don't like big cities. I don't like big cars. I don't like big houses. So, Italy is the perfect place for me."* Miuccia Prada, Italian fashion designer, interview with Suzy Menkes, Vogue (2013)

- ☞ *"The Italians have a saying: Sex is like pizza. When it's good, it's really good. And when it's bad, it's still pretty good."* Unknown popular Italian saying

☞ *"You may have the universe if I may have Italy."*
Giuseppe Verdi, Italian opera composer

Venice Canals, Italy

LANGUAGE

LINGUA

Living abroad has never been easier with the growing number of younger generations speaking English and the many translating apps. However, in a country like Italy, where few citizens are fluent in a second language, the experience can translate into loneliness and isolation if you don't speak their language. Moreover, Italians tend to spend their whole lives in the same town they grew up in, meaning they may not be looking to form new friendships as they already have a well-established social circle. Consequently, immerse yourself in the Italian language and culture before you get there. Otherwise, it can be hard to forge new friendships, which might end up ruining your stay. Suppose you are already in Italy and still have difficulties mastering the basics of the language and can't afford private lessons; go to your town or city hall and ask for a list of the public centers offering foreigners free Italian classes.

Still, there are a few rules one needs to know when trying to learn the Italian language. One of them is that the Italian alphabet comprises only 21 letters: 5 vowels and 16 consonants. The letters J, K, W, X, and Y do not exist in Italian. What about Juventus? Will ask the soccer fans. Well, the name "Juventus" is derived from Latin and means "youth." That's because, even if those letters are not officially part of the alphabet, they are part of widely used foreign words (taxi, karaoke, weekend), number plates on cars, or made-up company names such as Juventus.

I once got lost in a small village in the province of Brescia, an hour away from Milan. I was with my brother and my husband. We were driving and lost our GPS signal. A group of young people came to our rescue, but unfortunately, none spoke English or French, and our Italian was very limited. Luckily for us, my husband had taken Spanish at school (I took German) and decided to try it as a last resort. A conversation between him talking in Spanish and the young men answering in Italian followed, and soon enough, we were back on track. Interestingly, Italian is said to be etymologically closer to French but linguistically more complex to learn for Italians than Spanish.

Today, more than half of Italians speak English, followed by French, Spanish, and German. And thanks to the increased number of expats, the many translation apps, cable, and the internet, you can live in Italy without ever learning the language. But remember that learning the basics of a language is a step towards integration and will play a role in how you interact with locals and how they perceive you. Not being fluent will also complicate navigating the local administration, house repairs, transportation, grocery shopping, etc., and influence how long you stay in the country, especially if you are alone.

Unlike English, Italian is highly gendered; nouns are either masculine (*il*) or feminine (*la*); there is no word for "it" in Italian. The gender is determined by the gender of the word referred to. For example, the tree (*il albero*) is masculine, while the flower (*la fiora*) is feminine. Unfortunately, no rule tells you which words are feminine or masculine, the same as in French, Portuguese, or Spanish, even though Italians use more articles than Spanish. My only advice is that every time you learn a new word, learn the gender simultaneously because, contrary to English, Italian has seven definite articles (*lo, il, la, l', gli, i,* and *le*) all translated by "the," and four indefinite articles "*un, un,' uno* and *una*" translated by "a" or "an" in English.

"*Una*" ("a" or "an" in English) is the indefinite article for feminine singular nouns. However, because of the rules of Italian grammar, "*un'*" is the contraction of "*una*" when it is followed by a word that starts with a vowel sound or a silent "h." This is done for phonetic reasons to make the language flow more smoothly. So, "*un' amica*" is used for "a female friend" because "*amica*" starts with a vowel sound (a). If the word begins with a consonant sound, you will use "*una*" instead, like "*una ragazza*" (a girl) or "*una macchina*," pronounced mah-kee-naha, car in English. Also, when writing or saying words in Italian, one should pay attention to accents because they can change the meaning of a word, like "*Pésca*" (peach, the fruit) and "*Pesca*" (fishing, the action).

It is important to note that Italians do not add an "s" (or "x") to form the plural. Instead, for masculine words ending with "a," "e," and "o," you will change the vowels into an "i" in plural form. For instance, "*il bambino*" (the boy) becomes "*i bambini*" (the boys). Feminine words ending with "a" like "*la ragazza*" become "*e ragazze*" (the girls) in the plural form, with the "a" switching to "e."

"You" can be translated by *"tu," "lei,"* or *"voi." "Tu"* – singular and informal – is used when addressing friends, family members, or people of the same age group. *"Voi"* – plural and informal – is used when addressing two persons or more. In some regions, especially in the South, it is still used to show politeness to an older person or a stranger. *"Lei"* – formal but singular – is also used when addressing one person formally or politely but is commonly used in professional settings or with individuals who deserve a certain level of respect.

> **Note**: If you like listening to parodies of accents, you might find "The Italian Man Who Went to Malta" amusing. You can search for it on Google or YouTube. Though some may consider it vulgar, I find it hilarious.

Words that look similar in two languages but have different meanings are called "false friends." Here are some examples of "false friends" between English and Italian words:

- *Actual* is real or existing in English, while *"Attuale"* means current or present in Italian.

- A *library* is a place where you borrow books from in English. On the other hand, *"Libreria"* is a bookstore or bookshop in Italy. A library is *"una biblioteca"* in Italian.

- *Sympathy* (English) and *"Simpatia"* (Italian). While they sound similar, in English, sympathy refers to feelings of pity or compassion, whereas in Italian, *"simpatia"* refers to friendliness or likability.

- ☞ The *camera,* a device used to take photos, becomes room (*Camera*) in Italian.

- ☞ A "*Parente*" is a relative in Italy. The word for parents is "*genitori*" in Italian. A genitor is someone's biological father in English, not to be mistaken for a janitor or a custodian.

- ☞ *Fabric* refers to the material used for making clothes in English, while "*Fabbrica*" means factory in Italian. The word for fabric is "*il tessuto*" or "*la stoffa*" in Italian.

- ☞ To *pretend* is "to act as if something is true when it's not" in English, whereas "*Pretendere*" means to expect or claim something in Italian.

- ☞ *Sensible* means full of common sense, practical or reasonable in English, but "*Sensibile*" generally means sensitive in Italian.

- ☞ What Americans call *Pepperoni* - a type of sausage used to make pizza - is called "*Salami*" in Italy and most of Europe. "*Peperoni*" are bell peppers in Italy.

- ☞ While you will call an attractive young woman "*Bimbo*" in English, the word means young boy in Italian.

Limoncello in Grappa Wineglasses

DATING IN ITALIAN

Appuntamenti In Italiano

The story of an Italian mother who won a court order to evict her two adult sons, whom she called "*Bamboccioni,*" or "Big Babies," made headlines because the two men, both in their forties, lived at home without contributing financially despite being employed. Although surprising to some, this phenomenon is not new to Italy, where young adults tend to live with their parents longer than their Scandinavian or American peers, for example. This is partly due to cultural norms and the low wages that make rent unaffordable. However, these living arrangements often allow the children to save enough money to buy a home. So, if your date is still living with Mom and Dad, it's likely that it will be to get their own place when they do move out.

Here are some useful expressions if you meet that special someone:

- *"Vorresti uscire con me?"*: Would you like to go out with me?
- *"Ti va di andare al ristorante?"*: Would you like to go to a restaurant?
- *"Posso offrirti qualcosa da bere?"*: Can I offer you something to drink?
- *"Ti piacerebbe rivederci?"*: Would you like to meet again?
- *"Dove vuoi andare?"*: Where would you like to go?
- *"Dove vivi?"*: Where do you live?
- *"Che lavoro fai?"*: What do you do for a living?
- *"Che cosa ti piace fare nel tempo libero?"* What do you like to do in your free time?
- *"Sei molto carina"* (female): You are very pretty.
- *"Sei molto carino"* (male): You are very handsome.
- *"Ho passato una serata molto piacevole"*: I had a great time.
- *"Ti piacerebbe rivederci?"*: Will I see you again?
- *"Bella/ bellissima ragazza"*: beautiful / gorgeous girl
- *"Cin cin"*: Cheers!
- *"La vita e piu dolce con te!"*: Life is sweeter with you!
- *"Appuntamento"*: Appointment, Date, Rendezvous

- "*Caro*" (masculine) / "*Cara*" (feminine): Dear
- "*Tesoro mio*": My treasure, darling, sweetheart
- "*Piccola*" (feminine) / "*Piccolo*" (masculine): Small, Cute, or Babe
- "*Il fidanzato*": the boyfriend
- "*La fidanzata*": the girlfriend
- "*Figo*" (masculine) / "*Figa*" (feminine): Cool / Attractive
- "*Bello*" (masculine) / "*Bella*" (feminine): Handsome / Beautiful

I remember explaining to an American friend that calling one's love "*puce*" in French, which translates to "*flea*" in English, wasn't derogatory or unusual as a term of endearment, just like "*kawaii tamago*," "cute egg," in Japanese, or even "*honey*" in English. So, if your Italian date calls you the following words, that means they like you since they all translate as "Sweetheart," "Darling," or "Babe."

- "*Cucciola*" (feminine) / "*Cucciolo*" (masculine): Puppy
- "*Pulcino*" (masculine) / "*Pulcina*" (feminine): Chick/baby bird
- "*Passerotto*" (masculine) / "*Passerotta*" (feminine): Little sparrow
- "*Gattina*" (feminine) / "*Gattino*" (masculine): Kitten

- *"Topolina"* (feminine) / *"Topolino"* (masculine): Little mouse
- *"Polpetta"* (feminine) / *"Polpetto"* (masculine): Meatball

COMMON EXPRESSIONS IN ITALIAN:
Espressioni Comuni In Italiano

- *"Ciao"*: *Hi/Bye!* You say it to greet or say goodbye to relatives, close friends, young children, or young people. Not to be said to anyone you haven't met before or are not familiar or close with. Otherwise, a simple *"Buonjourno"* (Good morning) would be more appropriate. Italians value politeness and respect, so there is no better way to make a good first impression than using the correct greeting.
- *"Permesso"*: *Can I?* You use it to ask for permission or consent to do something or go somewhere. You also use it before entering someone's house, even if invited.
- *"Buongiorno a tutti"*: *Good morning, everyone!*
- *"Buon pomeriggio"*: *Good afternoon*
- *"Buona sera"*: *Good evening*
- *"Buona note"*: *Good night*
- *"Salve"* (more formal than *"Ciao"*): *Hello/Goodbye*
- *"Arrivederci"*: *Goodbye*

- *"Pronto"*: *Ready.* You can also use it when answering the phone. It originates from when telephone calls happened through operators. They would say *"Pronto"* to let the person know the connection was "ready." In some cases, it can also mean *"Hello"*.
- *"Scusi"*: *Excuse me*
- *"Mi chiamo..."*: *My name is...*
- *"Como si chiama"*: *What's your name?*
- *"Posso avere..."*: *Can / May I have...*
- *"Cuanto?"*: *How much*
- *"Un bicchiere d'acqua, per favore"*: *A glass of water, please!*
- *"Grazie"*: *Thank you.*
- *"Sì"*: *Yes /* *"No"*: *No*
- *"Per favore"*: *Please*
- *"Ho bisogno di..."*: *I need (Ho bisogno di aiuto.: I need help.)*
- *"Grazie per il tuo aiuto."*: *Thank you for your help*
- *"Scusi, può dirmi dove si trova...?"*: *Excuse me, can you tell where is...?*
- *"Toilettes"*: *Bathrooms*
- *"Come stai" / "Come va"*: *How are you?*
- *"Sto bene, grazie. E tu?"*: *I'm good, thank you. And you?*

- *"Anch'io sto bene, grazie."*: I'm doing well too, thanks. (Anch'io: Me too)
- *"Tutto bene"*: All good / Everything's fine
- *"Scusa, parli inglese?"*: Excuse me, do you speak English?
- *"Buona fortuna"*: Good luck!

COMMON VOCABULARY WORDS IN ITALIAN:
Parole Comuni Del Lessico Italiano

- *"L'uomo"*: The man / *"La donna"*: The woman
- *"Il ragazzo"*: The boy / *"La ragazza"*: The girl
- *"Un amico"*: a (male) friend" / *"Un'amica"*: a female friend or girlfriend
- *"La città"*: The city
- *"Signore"* / *"Signora"*: Sir/Madam
- *"La casa"*: Home/house
- *"Pausa pranzo"*: Lunch break
- *"L' ospedale"*: The hospital
- *"Il albergo"*: The hotel
- *"Il fontaniere"*: The plumber
- *"Il cane"*: The dog
- *"La polizia"*: The police

COMMON SLANG EXPRESSIONS IN ITALIAN:
Espressioni Gergali Comuni

- *"Che figata!"*: How cool!
- *"Che palle!"*: How boring! What a pain!
- *"Non ci piove"*: Of course!
- *"Dai"*: Come on! Let's go!
- *"Boh"*: I don't know (I dunno)
- *"Magari"*: Maybe / I wish
- *"Ottimo"/"Fantastico"*: Great / Fantastic!
- *"Favoloso" / "Incredibile"*: Awesome!
- *"Che fregatura!"*: What a rip-off!
- *"In bocca al lupo"*: Good luck, Break a leg!
- *"Figurati!"*: Don't worry about it! No need to!
- *"Vecchia"*: Old lady (slang for mom)
- *"Vecchio"*: Old man (slang for dad)
- *"Mannaggia"*: Damn!
- *"Devo filare"*: Gotta run!
- *"Che cavolo"*: Geez, What the hell!
- *"Cascasse il mondo"*: No matter what!
- *"Assolutamente" / "Completamente"*: Totally!
- *"Che succeede?" / "Come va?"*: What's up!

Carnival Mask, Venice, Italy

COMMON VERBS IN ITALIAN

Verbi Comuni In Italiano

You can't speak a language correctly if you haven't learned to conjugate it. Remember that the ending of a conjugated verb in Italian changes based on its subject.

THE SUBJECT PRONOUNS ARE:

- *"Io"*: I
- *"Tu"*: You (singular, informal)
- *"Lui/Lei/Lei"*: He/She/You (singular, formal)
- *"Noi"*: We
- *"Voi"*: You (plural, informal)
- *"Loro/Loro"*: They/You (plural, formal)

SOME USEFUL CONJUGATED VERBS:

- *"Essere"*: to be *(Lo sono, Tu sei, Lui/lei/Lei è, Noi siamo, Voi siete, Loro/Loro sono)*
- *"Avere"*: to have *(Lo ho, Tu hai, lui/lei/Lei ha, Noi abbiamo, Voi avete, Loro/Loro hanno)*
- *"Fare"*: to do/make *(Lo faccio, Tu fai, Lui/Lei/Lei fa, Noi facciamo, Voi fate, Loro/Loro fanno)*
- *"Dire"*: to say/to tell *(Lo dico, Tu dici, Lui/Lei/Lei dice, Noi diciamo, Voi dite, Loro/Loro dicono)*
- *"Andare"*: to go *(Lo vado, Tu vai, Lui/Lei/Lei va, Noi andiamo, Voi andate, Loro/Loro vanno)*
- *"Venire"*: to come *(Lo vengo, Tu vieni, Lui/Lei/Lei viene, Noi veniamo, Voi venite, Loro/Loro vengono)*
- *"Capire"*: to understand *(Lo capisco, Tu capisci, Lui/Lei/Lei capisce, Noi capiamo, Voi capite, Loro/Loro capiscono)*
- *"Parlare"*: to speak/talk *(Lo parlo, Tu parli, Lui/lei/Lei parla, Noi parliamo, Voi parlate, Loro/Loro parlano)*
- *"Mangiare"*: to eat *(Lo mangio, Tu mangi, Lui/Lei/Lei mangia, Noi mangiamo, Voi mangiate, Loro/Loro mangiano)*
- *"Bere"*: to drink *(Lo bevo, Tu bevi, Lui/Lei/Lei beve, Noi beviamo, Voi bevete, Loro/Loro bevono)*
- *"Partire"*: to leave *(Lo parto, Tu parti, Lui/Lei/ Lei parte, Noi partiamo, Voi partite, Loro/Lore partono)*

Santa Lucia, Naples, Italy

MOVING TO ITALY

TRASFERIRSI IN ITALIA

TAKE A MOMENT

In the grand tapestry of life, our next chapter takes us to far-off horizons and regions as you embark on a new adventure: moving to Italy. I am thrilled to share this exhilarating journey with you and would like to invite you to play a special part in this chapter.

Just as you pack your bags and bid farewell to the familiar, I am reminded of the incredible journey my book has gone on since its beginning. Like you, it has crossed borders and transcended boundaries, resonating with readers worldwide. And now, I am asking for your help to continue its remarkable voyage.

As an author, I pour my heart and soul into the books I write, weaving the fibers of my resourcefulness into the pages you hold. I understand the transformative power of words and the significance of your unique perspective. That's why I invite you to leave a review for this book as a piece of the adventure you are ready to embark on. Your review is not merely a collection of words; it is a footprint and inspiration. It tells the world about your experience, thoughts, and emotions and shares a slice of the world this book has unlocked for you.

Whether you pen a brief note or craft an intricate review, your contribution, no matter how succinct or comprehensive your words are, will guide fellow explorers who have yet to discover Italy. Know that your review has the potential to touch souls and ignite passions. So, to join me in this next chapter, please visit my book's page by scanning the QR code or another source where you found the book, and share your thoughts.

As you dive into this new adventure of moving abroad, I am reminded that, in the end, it's the connections we make, the stories we share, and the adventures we take that truly define our lives. I hope that you'll be part of my story, just as I am a part of yours. Thank you for being supportive and helping me make your journey abroad an enriching and unforgettable experience.

GENERAL RULES

Regole Generali

You don't need a visa to move to Italy as an EU citizen. All you need to do is register at the Registry Office (*Anagrafe*) of your local town, city hall, or municipality (*Comune*).

WHAT EU CITIZENS NEED TO REGISTER AT THE REGISTRY OFFICE:

- ☞ Rental contracts/agreements (tourist rentals are not accepted) or Title Deeds
- ☞ Bank statements
- ☞ Private health insurance
- ☞ Job contract (if applicable) or "*Partita. Iva*" for self-employed individuals

However, if you are **not an EU citizen**, check with the Italian embassy or consulate in your home country for the most up-to-date information on visa requirements before traveling to Italy. If you plan to live long-term in Italy, it's essential to understand and know how to navigate the system. If you can afford it, consult a specialist in Italian Immigration Law or a legal representative. They will help you determine which visa is best for you and guide you through the process.

> **Note**: When applying for a visa, allow enough time for the visa application process. Give yourself some time and try to apply at least six months before your intended departure time.

The Electronic Visa Application System (EVAS) allows citizens of certain countries to apply for a Schengen Visa online for short-term stays of up to 90 days. Check with the Italian consulate or embassy in your home country to see if they offer the service.

> **Note**: Short-term stays last up to 90 days within 180 days.

If you need a visa, you must apply in person at the Italian consulate or embassy in your home country. Even if you do the visa application online, you must still appear in person to provide biometric data and the required documents. If you have hired a lawyer, they will take care of everything, and they might accompany you to the appointment where you will submit your documents and attend an in-person interview. Sometimes, you must legalize certain documents, which can be done through an Apostille Stamp or at the Italian embassy. Call your local embassy and ask questions if you need help or clarification.

> **Note:** The documents provided should be in English or Italian. Otherwise, have them translated by a certified translator.

Suppose you are a relative (dependent, child, parent) or a partner (spouse or legally registered partner) of a European Union (EU) or European Free Trade Association (EFTA) national. In that case, you can also move to Italy under the same rights to live, work, receive education, and access social security benefits as your European relative.

> **Note:** EFTA countries are Iceland, Liechtenstein, Norway, and Switzerland.

It is recommended to have good health insurance covering at least €30,000 in medical and hospital expenses when visiting Europe, even for a short period. This also applies to Italy. Even if you are moving to Italy, you will still need Private Health Insurance before accessing Italy's National Healthcare System.

Whether visiting or relocating to Italy, learning the language and being familiar with Italian culture will help you navigate daily life and interact with locals. The Italian housing market can be competitive, so try to find housing even before you relocate. Find a local real estate agent or use online resources to find apartments or houses for rent or purchase.

Italy has an extensive transportation system, including trains, buses, and metros. Understanding how to navigate Italian public transport systems is important, even more so if you don't plan to own a car. However, if you need a car, consider the cost of buying one in Italy versus shipping the one you already have.

SHIPPING YOUR CAR TO ITALY

Spedire La Vostra Auto

If you choose to ship your car, make sure it meets Italy import eligibility criteria, including emission standards, vehicle age restrictions, and other requirements and restrictions such as customs fees or value-added taxes. Most shipping companies will ship your car by sea; just make sure it is clean and leave no personal belongings inside. Remember to take detailed pictures of the car's condition for the insurance in case of damage or loss. Also, examine the pros and cons of moving with your car vs. buying one in Italy. And sometimes, depending on where you intend to live, having a car might not be worth it because of limited parking options, a wide choice of transportation means, proximity to all the amenities, local taxes, etc. Try to consult an import and customs specialist for more guidance.

As stated above, you should consider the costs before shipping your car to Italy. Many major Italian dealerships offer electric models, from compact to SUVs and luxury vehicles, so you won't be stuck driving a stick shift or manual car if you choose not to. Once in Italy, you must register your vehicle by paying registration fees, obtaining Italian license plates, and having local insurance, so make sure you take the vehicle registration documents, proof of ownership, and insurance records, if applicable. You can drive your car in Italy for six months before registering it. If you owned your vehicle for over a year, you could import it duty-free six months after receiving your Residence Permit. You will then register your car at the Vehicle Registration Office, "*Pubblico Registro Automobilistico*" (PRA), and get Italian license plates.

A Trabucco Structure, Chieti, Italy

INTERNATIONAL MOVING AND SHIPPING COMPANIES

Società Di Traslochi E Spedizioni Internazionali

If you plan to import any personal belongings to Italy, familiarize yourself with the import regulations and requirements by contacting the Italian embassy or consulate in your home country. Household goods may be imported duty-free within six months of receiving Italy Certificate of Residence or Residence Permit.

> **Note**: The requirements and procedures for importing personal belongings to Italy may vary depending on your country of origin and the nature of your move.

You should gather all the necessary documentation and make an inventory list of your belongings before exploring the different shipping options for transporting, like container shipping and roll-on/roll-off (RoRo) services. Reach out to international moving companies with experience in relocating goods to Italy, request quotes, and compare services and prices before picking one since importing household items without customs complications can be made easier with the help of a trustworthy and experienced shipping agent. They can provide guidance on the logistics, shipping options, customs requirements, and necessary documentation for transporting your personal belongings and car. Depending on your country of origin, it might be a good idea to consult with your insurance provider to see their international coverage options or requirements for damage caused to your personal belongings.

MOVING WITH CHILDREN IN ITALY
Trasferirsi In Italia Con I Bambini

Even though children are resilient and adjust quickly, they will be affected whenever there is change. If you have children, let them know what is happening, no matter their age. You should have honest and open communication with them, and answer their questions the best you can, especially with teenagers, and plan with them. If you can, travel with them to Italy before moving, let them pick the new house (consider proximity to school, parks, etc.), and see if they can visit their new school before the move. Ask the school if they can put you in contact with a family with children the same age before school starts or put them in a summer camp to get familiar with their new peers. This will reduce any anxiety and get them excited. Unless it's last minute, you should give them enough time to say goodbye to their friends. Also, don't ship their special belongings; pack them with you instead. Being surrounded by familiar things while waiting for the rest of their possessions to arrive will help if they become homesick. If your children are young, they will pick up the language quickly. However, if they are older, you might want them to take Italian lessons before the move. Even if they attend a private school in Italy, they will still need to know the language to take public transportation or make new friends by joining local clubs, sports teams, or community events. Make sure you have all their necessary documentation, including birth certificates, school records, and any medical records. These documents may be required for school enrollment and healthcare.

> **Note**: If you are a single parent or circumstances change, have legal guardianship arrangements in place for your children according to Italian regulations.

MOVING WITH ANIMALS
Trasferirsi Con Animali

MOVING WITH PETS

When my friend moved from Los Angeles to Japan with her cat, Bruce, she wasn't concerned about her beloved companion feeling homesick but how he would react to long-distance travel. If you are moving with a pet (*un animale domestico*), be sure your chosen airline company accepts animals, as not all do. Some companies will fly your pet in a plane cabin if they are small enough, which was the case for my friend and her cat, or if they are emotional support animals. However, since most animals will fly cargo, I advise buying a flexible flight ticket that will allow you to fly at the same time/day as your pet. Consider it an alternate insurance policy in case of cancellations because you can always change your dates and still travel with them. And if you can't travel on the exact dates as them, hire a shipping company that will make sure your four-legged friend is comfortable and safe, especially if there are any layovers. You don't want to run the risk of them being left behind or, worse, being lost.

> **Note**: Some shipping companies will handle all the paperwork and ensure everything is done according to the Italian agricultural department's requirements.

Italy is a very pet-friendly country. Dogs are welcome everywhere: tourist sites, shops, restaurants, cafés, and even on public transport, where they must pay a small pet fee. However, big or unfriendly dogs must be kept on a muzzle or a leash. Some cities have even implemented silent fireworks for official events to counter the effect of loud noises on pets. Besides cats and dogs, parrots, geckos, land turtles, Indian blackbirds, Peruvian guinea pigs, ferrets, chinchillas, iguanas, and bearded dragons are the other pets allowed in Italy. Your local Italian embassy can also provide a list of the animals legally accepted in Italy, especially if your pet is a snake because not all of them are allowed in the country.

> **Note**: Your pet must be over three months old to enter Italy.

Your pet must be vaccinated, and the number of vaccines will depend on where you are traveling from and the kind of pet it is. Also, check in advance to see if your pet will be submitted to quarantine once they land in Italy. According to EU regulations, "to introduce animals in Italy from third countries, it is mandatory to obtain a European Community Veterinary Certificate for each pet that will be introduced in the Member States."

> **Note**: If your pet has no passport, an Italian vet can issue an EU Pet Passport. You will be expected to register your dog's microchip at the Dog Registry (*Anagrafe Canina*).

MOVING WITH LARGER ANIMALS

After reading my book about "Starting a New Life in Portugal," one of my readers from Canada reached out. She was an equestrian and was going to Portugal to train with Gilberto Felipe, the World Equitation Champion. I even got to "meet" her via Zoom, where we chatted for almost an hour. She had an exciting life, and I enjoyed talking with her. Even though it makes perfect sense, we rarely hear about people traveling with large animals. Therefore, if you are planning to move to Italy with a big or large animal, start by familiarizing yourself with Italian regulations and requirements for animal importation, as they might vary based on the region of Italy you are entering. The transport crates or trailers must meet international travel standards for animal transportation and be prepared for your animal to undergo quarantine and inspection upon arrival in Italy. When choosing a transport company, make sure they are professionals with international large animal transportation experience because you want to guarantee your animal's journey is safe, comfortable, and compliant with all regulations. Also, be sure you can communicate effectively with the company, veterinary authorities, and any other parties involved. Also, depending on your country of origin, there might be specific health checks, tests, and vaccinations that your animal will need to undergo before travel.

> **Note**: Consider any specific needs your animal may have during the journey, such as feeding, watering, and rest stops, and plan the travel route accordingly to minimize stress.

WHAT YOUR ANIMAL NEEDS TO TRAVEL TO ITALY:

- Identification microchip
- Up-to-date rabies vaccines, 21 days before the travel date if the pet's first vaccine
- Accredited vet issued health certificate
- A carrier or kennel (labeled with the owner's name, address, and contact number)
- Travel documents, crate or trailer, and import permits for larger animals, if applicable

> **Note**: Your pet won't need tick or echinococcus treatments to enter Italian territory, but carrying a tick-removal kit can't be a bad idea.

PROS OF LIVING IN ITALY
Vantaggi Della Vita In Italia

- Rich cultural history, art, and architecture
- Access to prestigious universities and various scientific and technological fields
- Chance to savor authentic Italian food and explore regional specialties
- High quality of life: beautiful landscapes, enjoyable climate, and a relaxed lifestyle
- Lots of cultural events, outdoor activities, and a strong sense of community

- ☞ A convenient base for traveling to other European countries
- ☞ Reasonable living costs in many regions (compared to other Western European countries)
- ☞ Career opportunities
- ☞ Strong economy compared to most countries

CONS OF LIVING IN ITALY
Aspetti Negativi Della Vita In Italia

- ☞ Need of a visa for non-European citizens
- ☞ For people with a low budget, Italy can be relatively expensive compared to European countries like Portugal, especially if you stay in cities like Rome or Milan
- ☞ Limited internet connectivity in remote areas or small towns
- ☞ Cold and rainy winters, depending on the region
- ☞ Language barrier, especially if you must deal with the bureaucracy
- ☞ Some people pointed out that Italians tend to reject anything that is not Italian, hence the importance of learning the language, etiquette, customs, etc.

Naples, Italy

ITALIAN ENTRY REQUIREMENTS
REQUISITI D'INGRESSO ITALIANI

The documents you must present at the Italian port of entry depend on your nationality or citizenship. After checking your documents, if the Italian Border Officer concludes that you are not a risk for Italy, you will be permitted to enter the country and thus the Schengen Territory. If you are entering Italy from a non-Schengen country or a country outside the European Union (EU), do not be surprised if the Italian border authorities stamp your passport despite the rise of digital checking.

> Note: The Border Officer makes the final decision on whether you shall be permitted to enter Italy or not.

ETIAS

European Travel Information and Authorization System

All visa-free travelers from outside the Schengen Area who wish to travel to Italy for a maximum stay of 90 days within 180 days must complete a simple online application to receive a mandatory visa waiver or an ESTIAS (European Travel Information and Authorization System). The authorization, which aims to increase security by pre-screening all visa-exempt travelers, is linked to the passport and valid for three years

ITALIAN ENTRY REQUIREMENTS | REQUISITI D'INGRESSO ITALIANI

from the date of approval unless the passport expires before the waiver, so make sure your passport is valid during the duration of the waiver. Unlike visa applications, approving an ETIAS application only takes a few minutes. If you are found ineligible for the waiver or your application is denied, you will apply for a Schengen visa instead. To find out whether you are eligible for an ETIAS, check their website since those who do not have a valid pass will be refused entry to Italy (and consequently the Schengen Zone).

HOW TO APPLY FOR AN ETIAS PASS:

To apply for an ETIAS authorization or pass, visit their website: www.etias.com . Otherwise, applicants will need to provide the following information and documents:

- Last or Family name at birth
- First name, date, place or country of birth, sex/gender, current nationality
- Current address
- Passport or travel documents
- For dual citizenship, information about your other nationality
- Valid email address and telephone number
- Name of the Schengen member state you first wish to visit or which EU country you will visit first if you intend to visit more than one EU country

(remember that all EU countries are not part of the Schengen Area)

☞ Education or job information

☞ ETIAS will run a background check and ask questions that will determine your eligibility (medical condition, criminal history, travel to warzone countries, any previous immigration or travel ban from an EU country...)

☞ For minors, the identity of the person responsible for them

☞ If the application is submitted by a person other than the applicant, the identity of the person and company that they represent, if applicable

☞ Proof of family ties for family members of EU citizens or residents (have your EU relative send you a copy of their ID)

> **Note:** Travelers under the age of 18 or over the age of 70 are exempted from paying the ETIAS fee.

SCHENGEN AREA / ZONE
Zona Schengen

Out of the 44 countries on the European continent, 27 of them are member states of the European Union: Austria, Belgium, Bulgaria, Croatia, the Republic of Cyprus, the Czech Republic, Denmark, Estonia, Finland, France, Germany, Greece, Hungary, Ireland, Italy, Latvia, Lithuania, Luxembourg, Malta, Netherlands, Poland,

Portugal, Romania, Slovakia, Slovenia, Spain, and Sweden. Since Brexit, British citizens can no longer move freely within the European Union (EU) and the European Economic Area (EEA). However, like most nationals from other European countries, they do not need a visa for short-term visits to Italy.

> **Note:** EEA countries include all EU countries plus three non-EU countries: Iceland, Liechtenstein, and Norway.

"The Schengen Area is the largest visa-free zone" where people can travel passport-free within participating EU countries: Austria, Belgium, Czech Republic, Denmark, Estonia, Finland, France, Germany, Greece, Hungary, Italy, Latvia, Lithuania, Luxembourg, Malta, Netherlands, Poland, Portugal, Slovakia, Slovenia, Spain, Sweden, with Bulgaria and Romania being the last to join, plus the four EFTA countries (Iceland, Liechtenstein, Norway, and Switzerland). "The EFTA (European Free Trade Association) is an intergovernmental organization that promotes free trade and economic cooperation among its four member states and operates independently of the European Union." As a side note, Schengen is the name of a small in Luxembourg, where the Schengen Agreements were signed in 1985.

Remember that although a member of the EU, Ireland is not part of the Schengen Zone. The UK was never part of the Schengen Area and is no longer a member of the EU since Brexit. Even though San Marino and Vatican City are not part of the EU or the EEA, they are part of the Schengen area thanks to their connection with Italy, meaning you can enter them with an Italian visa because they follow the same visa rules. Ireland, Liechtenstein, and Norway might not be part of the EU, but they are part of the Single Market Trade that allows people to work, shop, travel, study, and retire anywhere in the EU.

> Note: All EU countries are part of the Single Market Trade, but not all are part of the Schengen Area.

Whether you need a visa or not to enter Italy will depend on your nationality, Italian immigration policies, and the purpose and duration of your trip. Suppose you have a European passport; you only need that or an Identification Card (ID) to enter Italy. However, if you don't have a European passport or your country doesn't have visa-free agreements with Italy, you must present a valid passport or a travel document with a valid visa, if applicable, at the Italian Port of Entry. The documents you need to apply for a visa will depend on the visa type, the purpose of your visit, and your country of origin. As stated earlier, try to apply for your visa at the most six months before your departure or two weeks at the latest. And since visa requirements and procedures can change, visit the official website of the Italian embassy or consulate in your home country for the most accurate and up-to-date information. If your visa is rejected, because it can happen, you can always appeal the decision, but you might need the help of a good lawyer.

> **Note**: To find out if you need a visa to Italy or not, go to
> https://vistoperitalia.esteri.it/home/en

PAPERWORK

Carta

"*Bisogna mettere tutto nelle mani dell'avvocato*" or "You must put everything in the hands of a lawyer" is an Italian saying meaning if you can afford an agent or an immigration lawyer for all the transactions, you should get one. They will help with bank accounts, housing, insurance, schools, translation of documents, the immigration process, and much more. All application forms can be obtained from the Italian embassy or consulate in your home country. Passports must be valid for at least six months from the intended departure date, with at least two blank pages for official use. In some instances, you might be required to provide copies of previous passports. If you are from a country with visa requirements for the Schengen area, you will be required to have travel insurance coverage. Legal guardians would sign the forms for all minors or incapacitated persons.

But first, try to gather as many documents as possible for each applicant before starting your visa application.

- ☞ Official translations of documents, if required
- ☞ Birth and marriage certificates
- ☞ Identity documents: passport, identity card, driver's license, etc.
- ☞ Social security cards, if applicable
- ☞ All vaccinations, medical, and dental records

- Insurance policies, if applicable
- Academic records and diplomas
- Trophies, awards, letters of recommendation, invitations, etc.
- Employment records
- Proof of residency (utility bills, bank statements, taxes, etc.)
- A living will if you have one
- Any document you deem necessary

Contact your Italian embassy or consulate for information about their requirements for:

- Visas and permits
- Passport picture size requirements
- Vaccines for family members
- Vaccines and quarantines for pets
- Restrictions or taxes on shipped household items
- Taxes for shipping your car
- Insurances
- Anything you need information about

If your documents are not in Italian or the official language of your country, you may need to have them translated. The translations should be certified or notarized to ensure their authenticity. Also, some public documents issued by government authorities, such as birth certificates, marriage certificates, diplomas, and certain legal documents, might need an Apostille (a governmental form of authentication) instead. Since each embassy has its own regulations, check with your local Italian embassy to determine which documents are eligible.

> **Note**: If you have many documents to translate, give yourself enough time before starting your visa application. Also, if your documents are in English, check to see if they still need to be translated into Italian.

Italy offers many types of visas that can fall under the Uniform Schengen Visa (USV) or Type C Visa category for travels that do not exceed 90 days or the Long Stay or National Visa (NV) category, also known as Type D Visa, for extended stays longer than 90 days. For example, you can apply for a Schengen Work Visa if you need to be in Italy for business purposes for less than 90 days or a Long Stay Work Visa if you need to stay longer or are relocating to Italy for work.

> **Note**: You will be deported if you overstay your visa and may be banned from entering the Schengen Zone for a while.

VISA-FREE ENTRY

Ingresso Senza Visto

Any foreigner who does not belong to the Schengen area must have a valid passport to enter Italy, whether they require a visa or not. If your country of origin has visa-free agreements with Italy for short-term stays or, as stated above, you have a European passport, you won't need a visa to travel to Italy and the other Schengen member states for up to 90 days within a period of 180 days.

> **Note:** You must apply for an **ETIAS** pass or authorization before traveling to Italy if you don't have a European passport.

AIRPORT TRANSIT VISA / TYPE A VISA
Visto Di Transito Aeroportuale (Tipo A)

This visa is for people whose country doesn't have bilateral or visa-free agreements with Italy and whose flight must stop in Italy or any other Schengen country. Several years ago, I coordinated a group of Australian teenagers traveling to France without adult supervision. They were 15-16-year-olds traveling together from Sydney to Paris and back. However, they had to transit through a third country during one return flight. Unfortunately, one of the teenagers didn't have Australian citizenship and needed a transit visa for that country. Her parents were Australian residents but nationals of a country that did not have visa-free agreements with the country of transit. All ended well, though. I booked her on the same flight she took to travel to France, which transited to a country where she didn't need a transit visa, and soon, she was happily reunited with her family. Even if your country has bilateral agreements with all Schengen member states, check your return tickets to ensure your flight doesn't stop in a country like the UK, where you might need a transit visa if your country of origin doesn't have bilateral agreements with the UK.

Night View, Varnazza, Cinque Terre, Italy

ITALY TEMPORARY VISAS
Visti Per Soggiorno Temporaneo

As opposed to Long-term or Long-stay Visas, Italy Temporary Visas comprise Schengen Visas, designed for individuals intending to stay in Italy for short-term visits, Family Reunification Visas for family members seeking to join a relative temporarily in Italy, Short Stay Work Visas for individuals planning to work in Italy for a short period, Short Stay Student Visas for students intending to pursue a short-term course or language program in Italy. The duration of Italy Temporary Visas usually varies based on the type of visa and the purpose of the stay.

SCHENGEN VISAS (USV) / TYPE C VISAS
Visti Schengen

Typically, when you apply for a Schengen visa, you will be issued a Uniform Schengen Visa (USV). So, Schengen Visa, Uniform Schengen Visa, Short Stay Schengen Visa, or Type C Visa all refer to the same visa. **It is for non-EU citizens traveling for a short period to a European Union country and whose country does not have a visa-free agreement with the Schengen states.** If you are not a citizen of the country you live in and are wondering if you need a Schengen visa, check with your country of citizenship to learn about their visa travel agreements with Italy.

> **Note**: The Uniform Schengen Visa can be issued for short-term visits such as tourism, studies, research, business, conferences, cultural, religious, sports events, medical, or family purposes.

Besides stating "Schengen States," your visa will also display the "Number of Entries." "Single-Entry Schengen Visa" means the holder may enter Italy or any other Schengen member state once. "Double-Entry Schengen Visa" means the Schengen visa holder may enter and leave Italy or the Schengen Area twice, and "Multiple-Entry Schengen Visa" means the Schengen visa holder may enter and leave Italy or the Schengen Area as many times as they wish.

Your Schengen Visa will also specify the "Length of Stay." The visa will be valid for 90 consecutive days within 180 days in the Schengen area if nothing is specified. Otherwise, there will be dates indicating the validity of the visa that can range from six months to five years. And no matter how many entries you are allowed, all combined entries cannot exceed 90 days.

> **Note**: A Schengen Visa won't give you access to the UK unless your country of citizenship has visa-free agreements with the UK.

Suppose you find a job after your initial 90-day stay or decide to live in Italy while self-employed. In any case, you must return to your country of residence and apply for the appropriate visa at your local embassy. Even if you start the applications while in Italy, you will still have to go back home to retrieve the visa. (see Chapters about "Working in Italy" or "Italy Self-employment visa.") Unless you are marrying an Italian citizen, it is very difficult to extend a short-stay visa, except for humanitarian reasons, such as asylum or refugee, which is when it becomes difficult and dangerous for you to return to your home country. The other reason would be if you had a single-entry Schengen visa but entered Italy later than your Entry date. You can't enter Italy or any other Schengen state before your Entry date. If you need an extension, apply at least one week before your visa expires. Otherwise, it might prove too difficult to do.

WHAT YOU NEED FOR A TYPE C SCHENGEN VISA:

- ☞ Completed visa application forms
- ☞ Travel authorization for minors or court decision, if applicable
- ☞ Valid passport or travel document
- ☞ Recent passport pictures for each applicant
- ☞ Travel itinerary (with flight reservations or travel bookings indicating your planned entry and exit dates from the Schengen Area)
- ☞ Proof of accommodation (hotel/hostel reservations, invitation letter if staying with friends or relatives, Airbnb confirmation email)
- ☞ Travel medical insurance, if applicable
- ☞ Evidence of sufficient financial means to support yourself and any accompanying family member during your stay (bank statements, work certificates, sponsorship letters, proof of employment, etc.)
- ☞ Supporting documents related to the purpose of your visit (invitation letter from a business partner, medical files, conference, sports or cultural event registration, tourist itineraries, etc.)
- ☞ If you are not a national of your country of residence, proof that you are legally living there (residence permits, green cards, visas, etc.)
- ☞ Processing Fees

Note: Additional documents may be required based on your specific circumstances. Interviews for Schengen visas are usually very rare.

EXEMPTED FROM SCHENGEN VISA FEES:

☞ Children under the age of six

☞ Family members of European Union (EU) or European Economic Area (EEA) citizens may be exempt from visa fees if they are traveling to join or accompany the EU/EEA citizen family member

☞ Diplomatic and official passport holders traveling for official purposes (government officials, diplomats, or members of international organizations may be exempt from paying visa fees)

☞ Nationals from countries that have provisions for fee exemptions or reductions for specific categories of travelers

Note: Since fee exemptions can vary from country to country and may be subject to change, you should check with the Italian embassy or consulate where you are applying for the visa to see if you are eligible.

SCHENGEN VISA WITH LIMITED TERRITORIAL VALIDITY (LTV)

Visto Con Validità Territoriale Limitata

Depending on the reason for your travel, they will put a sticker on your passport if there are any restrictions. "**A Schengen Visa with Limited Territorial Validity**

(LTV) is a specific type of visa that allows the holder to enter and stay only in the specific Schengen country or countries specified on the visa sticker." If "Schengen States" is written on the sticker, you may travel to all countries within the Schengen Area. If one or several country names are listed, you may only visit these countries within the Schengen Area.

> **Note**: Unlike a Regular or Uniform Schengen visa, which grants access to all Schengen member states, an LTV visa restricts the holder's movement to the countries designated on the sticker.

SEASONAL WORK VISA

Visto Di Lavoro Stagionale

Italy does not have a specific "Seasonal Work Visa" program like some other countries. However, they offer various types of Short-stay work visas and permits that individuals can choose from based on their specific circumstances. This type of visa is mostly used by people who perform temporary or seasonal employment, such as agricultural work. Furthermore, some countries have reciprocal agreements with Italy for Working Holiday Visas, typically aimed at young people who want to travel and work for a limited period in Italy.

FAMILY REUNIFICATION VISA

Visto De Ricongiungimento Familiare

Often referred to as a Family Reunion Visa, this type of visa allows family members to reunite with relatives who are already residing in Italy and may have been separated due to immigration, work, study, or other reasons. Eligible family members often include spouses, children, parents, and sometimes other close relatives. The visa application process is typically initiated and sponsored by the family member, who must be a legal resident or citizen of Italy. It's the EU relative's – commonly referred to as the sponsor – responsibility to contact the Italian authorities to learn about the specific requirements and conditions for family reunification visas, including financial criteria, accommodation arrangements, health insurance, language proficiency, proof of family ties, etc., and submit all the application forms and supporting documents.

LONG-STAY OR "NATIONAL" VISA" (NV) / TYPE D VISAS

Visto Per Soggiorni Di Lunga Durata O "Visto Nazionale"

The Italy National Visa, another term for the Italy Long-Stay Visa, is **a generic visa for staying in Italy for over 90 days.** Currently, there are around 21 visas available, categorized into work/employment and non-working purposes. Non-working purposes include study, research, family reunification, medical treatment, religious reasons, retirement, etc.

A limited number of Long-Stay visas are issued annually for entrepreneurs, self-employed people, or freelancers (see the chapter about "The Nomad Visas" to learn more). This is important to remember because meeting the application deadline and submitting all necessary documents does not guarantee that you will get the visa you are applying for since the number of applicants sometimes exceeds the number of visas available, resulting in a waiting list. I experienced this when I applied for a US Work Visa. I later found out that there was a quota for my visa category, and unfortunately, I missed out. I had already quit my job and given up my apartment when I got the news. Even though I got it the following year, this experience taught me the importance of planning and giving yourself enough time, especially if you have a family (which wasn't my case) or dependents. (To learn more about Italy's Work Visa, see the chapter about "Working in Italy.")

The type of Long-stay visa you get will depend on your country of origin, the purpose, and the length of your stay because **each type of visa has specific requirements and application procedures.** Remember that Temporary or Short-stay work visas, study visas, family reunification visas, and so on can all be turned into Long-Stay visas if the length of stay exceeds 90 days or three months. Some visas may be valid for just a year or more, while others might need to be renewed periodically. The only Italian visa that can't be renewed is the tourist visa.

> **Note**: Elective Residence Visas are categorized as Long-Stay visas. (see the chapter about "Retiring in Italy.")

WHAT YOU NEED TO APPLY FOR A LONG-STAY VISA:

This is a generic list, knowing that each visa category will require more specific documents related to the type of visa you are applying for.

- ☞ Completed application forms
- ☞ Valid passport or travel document
- ☞ Passport-sized photos
- ☞ Proof of accommodation
- ☞ Proof of financial means
- ☞ Health insurance coverage
- ☞ Any other required documents depending on your visa category

After you arrive in Italy with a Long Stay Visa, you will apply for a Residence Permit (*Permesso di Soggiorno*) within eight days. The Residence Permit allows you to legally reside in Italy for an extended period beyond the visa's initial duration. If your country has an embassy or consulate in Italy, remember to register yourself and your family with them. This way, they can always locate you in emergency or evacuation cases. Though Italy is a very safe country, it is also home to several active volcanoes, with the eruption of Mount Etna in 2019-2020 being the most recent.

> **Note:** Nationals from the UK will need to apply for a visa if they intend to live, work, study, or retire in Italy.

Limone, Lombardi, Italy

THE NOMAD LIFE
LA VITA DA NOMADE

Today, the word nomadism is an umbrella term that refers to the different aspects of the nomad lifestyle. For instance, nomadic tribalism usually comprises a group of people traveling together as a tribe. You might have met some living off-grid in their cars, vans, or RVs. Urban nomads are individuals or groups who lead a nomadic lifestyle within urban environments, like big cities, and often live a mobile or minimalist lifestyle. Digital nomads use technology to work remotely and travel continuously, constantly working from different locations around the world. Then, there are travel nomads who go from place to place, depending on their needs or wants. Seasonal workers usually fall under that category or people who would rather see the world than spend their lives at one given spot. I knew a guy who would show up in town every summer, stay for three months, and then disappear for the rest of the year. I once asked him what he was doing when he was not around. He explained that he was a surf instructor in the US during summer and a ski monitor in Europe during winter. The rest of the year, he would work on a farm or construction sites or travel the world. The last time I saw him, he was heading to Zanzibar, Africa.

If you are new to the nomadic lifestyle and are unsure if this life is right for you, let's first consider the pros and cons of nomadic life to help you decide.

WHY CHOOSE THE NOMAD LIFE
Perchè Scegliere La Vita Da Nomade

Living a nomad life means going places and learning about different cultures, lifestyles, and languages while making new friends. The lifestyle can even be beneficial for the whole family if done correctly. One of the biggest perks of becoming a nomad is the freedom to not be tied to an office counting the hours and no more time spent in traffic going to work. You become your own boss, setting up your own hours and schedule. Depending on your chosen country, you can enjoy great weather all year, save money, start a new life, or reinvent yourself. The chances of feeling isolated will be small because there is a vast network of nomads around the world ready to help.

WHAT ARE THE CONS OF A NOMAD LIFE
Quali Sono I Contro Di Una Vita Da Nomade

Unfortunately, there are quite a few cons to the nomadic lifestyle as well. Besides learning about visas and tax policies, you might need to use some of your savings if the costs of living end up being higher than what you are making. You should also be resourceful and ready to deal with the unexpected, such as illness, financial loss, death, inability to renew your visa, and so on. Or you might just become homesick because being away from home, making new friends, and keeping in touch with old ones can be challenging. The lifestyle might also prove more complicated than you thought, especially if you must move your entire family. If you are a digital nomad, your whole day will depend on Wi-Fi availability, and you will need to adjust your working hours depending on your time zone. And you will spend a lot of time in coffee shops, which, ironically, may also become your new office. Or you might not like the country or the lifestyle, which happens more often than people would like to admit, so always have a plan B.

FEW WAYS TO MAKE A LIVING AS A NOMAD IN ITALY

Alcuni Modi Per Guadagnarsi Da Vivere Come Nomade

If you're not self-employed and wondering how to make money in Italy as a nomad, ask yourself what you're good at. There is no better way to succeed than making money doing what you love. Otherwise, here are a few ideas:

- ☞ Start a travel blog (doesn't require any special skills)
- ☞ Sell your talents and become a moneymaker: knitting, painting, woodworking, carpentry, sewing, etc.
- ☞ Showcase your photography skills (even in the time of smartphones, there will always be a need for a good photographer)
- ☞ Do not disregard waitressing or bartending!

- ☞ Consider teaching your language as a second language. And if you can't find an institution offering it, be the one to suggest it (there will always be people who would rather learn from another human than an app)

- ☞ Volunteer. WWOOF, or "Worldwide Opportunities on Organic Farms, is a network that links volunteers to organic farms, where they work on the farm in exchange for food and accommodation. Here is the link: *https://wwoof.net*

- ☞ Become "a Workaway traveler who wants to give back to the communities and places they visit" through *www.workaway.info*

- ☞ Join the seasonal workers; go fruit picking; be a lifeguard, a ski instructor, a tennis instructor…

- ☞ Work in a hostel – no strings attached (you can leave whenever you want)

- ☞ Sitter: house sitter, babysitter, pet-sitter, garden-sitter (if it needs to be looked after, be that person)

- ☞ Or find an internship in your field

THE DIGITAL NOMADS
I Nomadi Digitali

When the Covid 19 Pandemic hit in 2020, it led to the rise of a new kind of nomadism: the Digital Nomad. During a trip to Alaska, I had the pleasure of meeting a young couple in their twenties traveling in their camper van and working remotely using Starlink for internet access. They had already explored the lower 48, a term used to refer to the 48 states of the United States, excluding Alaska and Hawaii. Even though they confirmed the belief that all digital nomads are some 20-year-old backpackers traveling the world with their MacBooks, fortunately, this is not always the case. Even if the average digital nomad is 34, many are over 40, and some are even in their sixties. There are as many men as women, the majority being White, followed by Hispanics/Latinos, Asians, and Blacks. Most work in information technology, followed by creative services, education and training, sales, marketing, PR, finance, accounting, and consulting. A smaller number are into coaching and research.

> **Note**: In most cases, people can't tell the difference between nomads and expats, even if expats are usually tied to a job and a location.

BEST JOBS FOR DIGITAL NOMADS
Lavori Migliori Per Nomadi Digitali

Freelance Writing and Content Creator – besides being a writer, you can create content for blogs, websites, and publications – Web Development and Design, Graphic Design, Online Teaching and Tutoring, Software Development, Virtual Assistance, Digital Marketing and SEO, E-commerce and Drop-shipping, Project Management, Affiliate Marketing, Consulting, Sales and Business Development, Digital Marketing, Healthcare (Telemedicine), Be part of Online Survey and Market Research, Customer Support, Cryptocurrency and Blockchain, Personal Coach or Mentor, Podcast Host,

Social Media and Community Manager, Short Videos Editor and much more.

Pienza, Tuscany, Italy

WHERE TO STAY AS A DIGITAL NOMAD IN ITALY
Alloggi Per Nomani Digitali In Italia

Most digital nomads stay in big cities like Milan, Florence, Venice, and, of course, Rome, the number one choice for digital nomads in Italy. Despite being a capital city, Rome remains quite affordable and makes it easier to run a business. It has high-speed internet, numerous co-working spaces, easy access to the rest of Europe, and hosts most embassies. If you are into fashion or are a creative person, Milan has everything a remote worker needs to be productive. Florence has some of the world's best museums and art galleries, and as one of the most visited cities in Italy, it is very welcoming to foreigners. However, digital nomads should also consider mid-size cities because they sometimes have the same advantages as big cities with less inconvenience.

Bologna, a safe mid-sized city, has fast internet and several coworking spaces. Not too crowded with tourists, it is perfect for digital nomads looking for a tranquil environment to live and work in. If you want to live in a romantic city, try the city of "Romeo and Juliet," Verona. It has many ex-pats and international students, giving it a friendly atmosphere. While the digital nomad scene in Genoa is not yet fully developed, the city offers everything a digital nomad needs. It is more affordable than other big cities, is safe, and has good internet speed. Despite the cost of living in Naples being a bit more expensive for the average digital nomad in Italy, the city offers a comfortable working environment with fast internet, internet cafes, and coworking spaces. If you are more of an introvert and want to avoid tourist crowds, head to the smaller historical city of Trieste, which has been attracting a growing number of digital nomads. Being a university city means Torino has a more affordable cost of living – and so does Palermo – besides offering an incredible nightlife scene. Digital nomads may also want to consider exploring smaller villages that are looking to attract new residents. For instance, Ollolai, a small town located in Sardinia, has created a program called "Work from Ollolai" with the aim of transforming the village into a hub for digital nomads.

Unless you own a property in Italy, you will need a temporary place to stay, at least until you find your own place. What you will pay for rent depends on which city or town you live in. Rentals – apartments, homes, or single rooms – are not the best options if you are on a budget or want the freedom to leave anytime, but they are perfect for families whose goal is to settle eventually in Italy. To find a home to rent in Italy, try Vrbo: https://www.vrbo.com/vacation-rentals/europe/italy. The website offers a list of vacation homes rented by homeowners and is perfect for families looking for a large house. Whenever I need to rent a house and find nothing on Airbnb, I always look into Vrbo. Like Airbnb, you can choose the length of your stay without committing to a fixed period. Some owners even list their houses on both sites simultaneously, even though Airbnb remains a practical and popular accommodation option because of the flexibility in their terms and conditions. To find an Airbnb in Italy, go to https://www.airbnb.com/italy/stays. Moreover, Airbnb has established local hubs in Italy through its "Live and Work Anywhere" initiative "to help support destinations to become the most desirable and remote-worker-friendly locations worldwide."

> **Note**: It is easier to rent short-term than long-term in Italy because of the laws that favor the renters, not the owner, and the high property taxes.

"Scattered or dispersed hotels," commonly known as "*Albergi Diffusi,*" are "the most sustainable hotels in Italy," according to Forbes.com. They can vary in size and style and provide a unique and charming way to experience Italian culture, history, and rural life because they are often found in more countryside or less-visited areas. Guests get to stay in authentic, sometimes renovated traditional buildings, like old houses or barns converted into guest rooms, common areas or lobbies for check-in, dining rooms for breakfast, and living rooms *(Piazze.)* Or you can choose to stay in a Pension Hotel (*Pensione*) or an inn (*Pensionato Albergo*), often family-run establishments that provide accommodations and sometimes meals to travelers. Compared to larger hotels, pension hotels offer a cozier and more personal atmosphere. They are commonly found in tourist areas and range from budget to upscale options.

Co-living Spaces are a modern form of housing where like-minded people share a living space. Other than the apartment or house being rented for a shorter period, it is not that different from living with roommates; everyone has separate bedrooms but shares common spaces and sometimes interests. To find a co-living space in Italy, go to *https://coliving.com/italy*.

If you don't mind strangers staying at your place or staying at theirs, "Home Exchange" can be a cost-effective way to explore Italy. The only catch is that you must find someone whose needs meet yours. It works best if you are flexible on the location. Even though I haven't used the website for Italy, I used it to discover other cities, and it has been a great experience each time. If you are curious and unfamiliar with this concept, here is a link to their Italian website: *https://www.homeexchange.com/home-exchange-italy*

Then, you have the Hospitality Exchange networks, which remain a great way to meet and interact with locals. Even though few people use Couchsurfing nowadays, others have emerged, such as Be Welcome *https://www.bewelcome.org* and Warm Showers, geared towards cyclists, *https://www.warmshowers.org*, both are available in Italy.

Capri, Italy

NOMADS VISAS

VISTI PER NOMADI DIGITALI

Most digital nomads who enter Italy visa-free would continue to work remotely while visiting the country before heading to the next one. However, some other nomads take advantage of entering Italy visa-free to find a job and settle, leaving the country every 90 days to travel in the Schengen area, coming back for another 90 days, and so forth, without the uncertainty of being readmitted at every departure and running the risk of being deported if authorities find out they have been living and working in Italy without legal authorization. There are several visas that nomads can use to work and live legally in Italy, the most used one being Work Visas for Self-Employment Individuals. To determine if you are eligible for Self-Employment visas, consult with legal and business professionals who specialize in Italy's Work Visas.

The type of Italy Self-Employment visa you are looking for can be hard to get due to the strict requirements, including demonstrating sufficient financial means, a viable business plan, and professional qualifications. As a self-employed individual, you may not have the same access to public services and benefits as someone employed by a company. This includes healthcare coverage and other social services. Moreover, managing the administrative requirements, including tax obligations, registrations, and compliance with local regulations, can be time-consuming and challenging. And though self-employment visas usually grant the same rights to family members, this may not be done as automatically as other types of visas since it will depend on which kind of self-employment visa you request. Suppose you have a spouse who wants to pursue a career while living in Italy. In that case, you should double-check and see if they need to apply for a separate visa in case being dependent on your visa prevents them from legally working in Italy.

There are many Freelancers (*Freelancisti*) or Self-employed (*Liberi Professionisti*) in Italy. If you are a non-EU resident planning to work as a freelancer or be self-employed in Italy, you will need to obtain the appropriate visa as well as a Residence Permit.

Freelancers or self-employed in Italy usually use the following visas:

- Work Visa for Self-Employed Individuals (*Lavoro Autonomo*)
- Start-up Visa (see the chapter "How to start a business in Italy")
- Investor Visa (*Visto Per Investitori*)
- Elective Residence Visa (*Residenza Elettiva*)

> **Note**: Digital nomads who work as freelancers may be eligible for the **Italy Nomad Visa** and should consult a legal representative to determine whether their work qualifies.

SELF-EMPLOYMENT VISAS

Visto Per Lavoro Autonomo

The Italian Work Visa for Self-Employment Individuals is a type of Long-Stay Visa or D Visa for people who are not from the EU or EEA and intend to start their own businesses or work for themselves while living in Italy. They can be professionals or people engaged in a specific activity, entrepreneurs, businesspeople, artisans, partners or consultants in Italian companies, artists, business managers, college professors, researchers, etc. It is important to note that you cannot apply for an Italy Self-Employment Visa anytime. Italy has an immigration policy called **Flow Decree** (*Decreto Flussi*), **a specific period during which non-EU nationals can apply for** Italian seasonal work, non-seasonal work, and **self-employment visas**. However, **there is also a quota** for the number of visas that will be issued. So, if you plan on getting a Self-Employment Visa, you should check with your local embassy for the annual "Flow Decree's Publication" to see who can apply, when to apply, and the list of documents to provide.

The steps to getting a Self-Employed Visa are almost the same as a Work Visa, meaning you must first obtain a Clearance or Permit (*Nulla Osta*) issued by the competent authority, usually the Chamber of Commerce (*Camera di Commercio*) in the city where you intend to reside in Italy. Therefore, you should first contact the local Chamber of Commerce where you plan to establish your activity and ask about their requirements and which type of Permit you need. Consulting directly with the local Chamber of

Commerce or relevant authorities will give you the most accurate and up-to-date information regarding your situation. For instance, if you want to open a boba or coffee shop, you might need Authorization from the Department of Health Services, where you need to operate your business, on top of registering your business with the Chamber of Commerce to get the appropriate Clearance. You may also need to register for Value Added Tax (VAT) and obtain a VAT number if you think your business will generate an annual revenue above a specific limit. If you plan to import classic or vintage American vehicles to Italy, you might need a wholesale dealer license, and so on. Additionally, it may also be helpful to consult with a local professional or legal advisor to assist with the process, especially if you face a language barrier.

Before submitting your application to the Chamber of Commerce, you will prepare a comprehensive business plan that outlines your occupation and show proof of sufficient funds to support yourself and your business activities. Once you have chosen the legal structure for your company, such as sole proprietorship, partnership, limited liability company, etc., you will register with the Business Registrar (*Registro delle Imprese*) through the Chamber of Commerce. The Business Registrar is a public register where business information is recorded and made available to the public. This is where you should also get the information about social security contributions for self-employed individuals. Once you have fulfilled the requirements and submitted the necessary documentation, the Chamber of Commerce will review your application and may issue a (*Nulla Osta*) or Clearance. You must also register with the Tax Registrar (*Registro delle Imposto*) to get a fiscal code (*Partita IVA*) for yourself and your business. This code is necessary for various administrative and fiscal purposes.

Keep in mind that you must get all authorizations and clearances in Italy while you are still in your home country, meaning that, unless you have someone who can do it for you, you might have to hire an immigration lawyer in Italy to submit all the applications on your behalf, according to the time limits and modalities prescribed by the Flow Decree. Now, suppose you have been living in Italy. Being in the country might facilitate the process, such as providing the necessary documents promptly to get your authorizations. However, you will still have to leave the country to retrieve the visa from your country's embassy.

You will apply for the visa at your country's Italian embassy or consulate only after you have received your Clearance and all the authorizations or certifications needed to start your activity in Italy. If you have one, you or your lawyer will begin by booking an appointment and downloading and completing the Italy Long-Stay Visa Application Forms from the consulate website. You will submit all the documents, originals, and copies in person (your lawyer might accompany you if you have hired one) and pay the Italy visa fees on the day of your appointment. If approved, the embassy or consulate will contact you when your visa is ready.

You will travel to Italy only after you have received your visa. You will have a few days, usually eight, to apply for a Residence Permit Card for Self-employment Individuals (Permesso di Soggiorno per *Lavoro Autonomo*) at the local Post Office where you will look for the Immigration Desk (*Sportello Amico*) (see the chapter about "Residence Permit"). After acceptance of your application, you and your family members, if you have any, will receive a renewable permit with an initial validity of two years from the Foreign Department (Ufficio Stranieri) of your local Italian Police Headquarters. The Permanent Residence Permit will be issued to you after five years of continuous residence in Italy. You can apply for Italian citizenship after ten years of legally living in Italy. (see the chapter about "Citizenship in Italy")

WHAT YOU NEED TO OBTAIN A "*NULLA OSTA*" FOR SELF-EMPLOYED INDIVIDUALS:

- Business plan (nature of the business, target market, financial projections, and how the company will contribute to the local economy)

- Financial statements (the exact financial requirements will vary according to the nature of your business, so check with the appropriate authority)

- Legal structure (sole proprietorship, etc.)

- Valid passport or residence permit

- Comply with zoning regulations and other requirements if you need to rent a space for your business

- Comprehensive health insurance or liability insurance if you are operating a business such as a spa, a coffee shop, etc.

WHAT YOU NEED FOR AN ITALIAN VISA FOR SELF-EMPLOYED INDIVIDUALS:

- Completed Long-stay visa application forms

- Passport pictures

- A clean criminal record

- Valid passport

- Proof of accommodation in Italy

- Clearance (*Nulla Osta*)

- Annual gross income (they will tell you the amount) made one year before the visa application (work contracts, freelance services to Italian clients or companies, etc.)

- Health insurance (should cover hospitalization or medical expenses in Italy for the first 30 days of your stay)

- Civic status documents, if applicable

- Processing fees

Suppose you are going to be a partner or a CEO of an already existing company; you will also need the following:

- ☞ Chamber of Commerce Business Registry
- ☞ Company's Registration number
- ☞ Document stating your role within the company
- ☞ Copy of an Official Declaration of Responsibility issued by the local County Labor Office (Direzione Territoriale del Lavoro) that clearly states that your role won't be a subordinate one
- ☞ Proof of salary

Grado, Italy

ITALY INVESTOR VISA

Visto Per Investitori

For those familiar with the Golden Visa, the Italy Investor Visa, also known as the Italy **Entrepreneur Visa,** is considered its equivalent since they share the same goal: attract foreign investors, primarily non-EU citizens. The Italy Investor Visa gives non-EU citizens a renewable two-year visa for making significant investments or donations and the freedom to travel to all Schengen zone countries without a visa for up to 90 days within 180 days. Italy has even introduced a unique tax system for those seeking that visa.

> **Note**: Real estate investment doesn't qualify for an Investor Visa in Italy.

There are several ways to apply for the Italy Investor Visa. You can:

- Buy Italian Government Bonds,
- Invest in an operating Italian company,
- Support an innovative startup, or
- Make a charitable donation for cultural, educational, or research purposes

You must have a clean criminal record to apply for this visa. Also, your investment or donation must go to one entity, though exceptions can be made, and you must show that your assets were legally acquired and can be transferable in your name. **The application process for the Italy Investor Visa is also done in two steps**: you will first apply online for a Certificate of No Impediment or Clearance *(Nulla Osta)* and then in person at the Italian embassy or consulate for your visa.

Once you have determined the type of investment you want to make and are sure you meet the eligibility criteria for that specific investment, you will apply for a Certificate of No Impediment *(Nulla Osta)* through the Ministry of Enterprises and Made in Italy's website *(Ministero delle Imprese e del Made in Italy)* at https://investorvisa.mise.gov.it. An Investor Visa Committee will assess your application and make an official decision within 30 days. Remember that the department or agency responsible for issuing the Certificate may vary depending on the investment you plan to make. Upon receiving your Certificate, you will be granted a six-month window to apply for the visa at your nearest Italian embassy or consulate.

You should have physical copies of all previously submitted documents and the visa application authorization when applying for the visa. You can't apply for a visa without getting your Certificate or Clearance first. The consulate might ask for more documents and will notify you once your visa application is approved. The visa will give you a two-year validity period, within which you can enter Italy, where you will visit the Police Headquarters in person to initiate the process of obtaining an Italian Residence Permit for an Investor Visa. You will have a three-month window from your Residence Permit application date to complete your investment or donation.

Failing to meet this requirement will result in the revocation of your visa.

You can renew your Residence Permit by applying at least 60 days before it expires through the online Investor Visa portal. The Italy Investor Visa Committee will again review your application and check if you have maintained your investment/donation. You can apply for long-term EU residency after five years of regular residency in Italy.

> **Note**: You must maintain your investment to renew and keep your visa throughout your stay in Italy. You can apply for Italian citizenship after ten years of living in Italy.

HOW TO APPLY FOR THE ITALY INVESTOR VISA:

You will first need to apply for the Italy Investor "*Nulla Osta*" by submitting the following documents electronically:

- Copy of your passport
- A Curriculum Vitae (CV) outlining your academic and professional background
- Proof of ownership of the investment/donation funds (bank statements with your name and available funds)
- Evidence that the funds are legal and transferrable (official letter from your bank or financial institution)
- Criminal record issued by relevant authorities in your country

- A concise description (maximum 1,000 words) of the investment/donation's nature and your previous experience as an investor or donor
- Confirmation of consent from the investment/donation recipient
- Declaration of Commitment specifying the investment amount and intended settlement location in Italy

Upon reception of the "*Nulla Osta,*" you will submit the following documents at the nearest Italian embassy or consulate for the visa:

- Copy of the Clearance and all original copies of the documents mentioned above
- Proof of accommodation in Italy
- Proof of income from the previous financial year, meeting the minimum threshold for healthcare expense exemption
- Passport-size photos
- Valid passport
- Proof of residence in your home country

> **Note**: All documents must be in Italian or English; otherwise, a certified translation must be included. To learn more about the Italy Investor Visa Program, go to https://investorvisa.mise.gov.it/index.php/en/investor-visa-how-it-works

For specific inquiries related to investment opportunities, programs, or committees in Italy, you may also consider contacting the Italian Trade Agency (AIT), the Ministry of Economic Development, companies specializing in Italy's law and investment policies, or your local Italian embassy.

DIFFERENCES BETWEEN ITALY SELF-EMPLOYED AND INVESTOR VISAS:

ITALY SELF-EMPLOYED VISA:

- For non-EU individuals who wish to establish and operate their business in Italy
- Comprehensive business plan outlining the nature and viability of the proposed business
- No minimum investment amount
- One-year initial visa, renewable for two more years
- Subject to regular tax regulations for businesses
- Applicants must have a clean criminal record
- Financial stability and resources

ITALY INVESTOR VISA:

- For non-EU individuals who want to make a significant financial investment or philanthropic donation in Italy
- A minimum of €250,000 investment for innovative start-ups, or €500,000 in Italian shares

- ☞ Investment can be in government bonds, established Italian companies, innovative startups, philanthropic causes, etc.
- ☞ Renewable every two years
- ☞ Eligible for a special tax regime targeted towards Investor Visa holders
- ☞ Applicants must have a clean criminal record
- ☞ Financial assets must be acquired legally, transferable, and in the applicant's name
- ☞ Real estate investment is not an option for this visa

> **Note**: Italy's Chambers of Commerce play a significant role in supporting businesses, including those with foreign investors. They also provide investors and entrepreneurs with information, services, and networking opportunities.

ITALY DIGITAL NOMAD VISA (IDNV)

Visto Per Nomadi Digitali In Italia

Since 2019, over 25 countries have created Digital Nomad Programs. Before Italy got its new own Digital Nomad Visa, digital nomads who wanted to live in the country used either a tourist visa (they didn't need to open a bank account in Italy for that, but they could also discover too late that they had been working illegally in a country they were supposed to be visiting) or Italy Self-employed Visas.

The Italy Nomad Visa, also called the Remote Work Visa, implemented in April 2024, **was specifically designed for professionals who can work remotely**

using the internet and technology. **To be eligible, applicants must have highly qualified work activities that require specialized skills, expertise, or credentials.** Investors and businesspeople who want to expand their activities in the Italian market, freelancers, highly skilled self-employed professionals, IT specialists, software developers, designers, writers, consultants, and employees working remotely for a company that is established outside of Italy can all apply.

Applicants must be citizens from a country outside of the EU or EEA and have at least an annual income three times the minimum level required for exemption from participation in healthcare costs, which is approximately 28,000 euros. They should also have comprehensive health insurance that covers their entire stay in Italy and provides protection for medical emergencies, illnesses, accidents, and unexpected healthcare expenses. Furthermore, they must conform to Italy's regulations and social security obligations and must comply with Italy's taxation requirements before applying for the visa, meaning the Italian Tax Office might contact their countries of origin tax offices to discuss their case. On the other hand, they will be exempted from getting a *"Nulla Osta,"* which should simplify the application process and reduce the processing time. Additionally, they won't be subject to the Flow Decree, which limits the number of foreigners who can apply for a visa. Once the visa is delivered, applicants will have 8 days after entering Italy to apply for a renewable residence permit at the Police Headquarters, which will assign them a tax code. They will also be required to get a VAT number from the Tax Office, which will be notified by the Police Headquarters upon issuance of the permit.

> **Note**: If you're an EU/EEA passport holder, you don't need an Italy Digital Nomad Visa to work remotely from Italy. However, if you plan to stay for more than three months or 90 days, you must declare your presence and get a Temporary Residency Certificate (usually valid for five years).

WHY GET AN ITALY DIGITAL NOMAD VISA:

- Free access to the Schengen Area
- Family Reunification
- Possibility to become Permanent Resident
- Exemption from getting a *"Nulla Osta"*
- Not subjected to the Flow Decree

CONS OF THE ITALY DIGITAL NOMAD VISA:

- Laborious application process
- Not accessible to all remote workers
- One-year renewable Residence Permit, providing applicants still meet the eligibility requirements
- Make it impossible to work for Italian companies
- The Police headquarters has the final word on family reunification
- Must have been a remote worker for a least six months before visa application
- Comprehensive 12 month-health coverage

WHAT YOU NEED FOR THE ITALY DIGITAL NOMAD VISA:

- Valid passport and ID
- Recent passport photos
- Proof of sufficient funds to cover your stay (income, bank statements...)
- Clean criminal record for the last 5 years
- Proof of comprehensive medical insurance
- Proof of accommodation
- For nomads working for a company registered and based outside of Italy, a valid work contract or agreement that outlines the terms and conditions of employment, including the nature of the work, duration, and compensation, or the annual gross income earned one year before the application
- Processing fees

> **Note**: Remember that as a digital nomad, you can still apply for an Investor, Self-employment, or Start-up Visa to live and work in Italy.

Todi, Umbria, Italy

WORKING IN ITALY
LAVORARE IN ITALIA

You will need a Work Permit to work in Italy if you are a non-EU/EEA citizen. However, you must first secure a job offer from an Italian employer. If your profession requires specific qualifications or licenses, you may need to have your credentials recognized or undergo an evaluation process to ensure compliance with Italian standards.

Remember that **there is a quota on the number of Italian Work Permits** available to foreign nationals. These quotas include spots reserved for:

- ☞ Certain nationalities in select professions (construction, tourism, telecommunications, etc.)
- ☞ People who already hold a Residence Permit in Italy or the European Union and want to change their status and apply for a Work Permit
- ☞ Students already living in Italy and who want to convert their Student Residence Permits into Work Residence Permits
- ☞ Self-employed individuals

You will reapply for a Work Permit each time you switch jobs, and your Work Permit must always match your job position or location. You can apply for Permanent Residence or Italian Citizenship after working and living in Italy for five to ten years.

> **Note**: Some work permits may require a health examination or medical certificate.

Working in Italy comes with some benefits depending on your job contract and length of work. First, workers in Italy are entitled to Paid Vacation Leave, typically 4 to 5 weeks per year, depending on their length of service and agreements. Italy has several national public holidays, the number of which may vary by region, and employees are generally entitled to paid time off.

> **Note**: Depending on the region, you might have to pay for regional taxes on top of national taxes. Remember when negotiating your work salary if you will be working for an Italian firm.

If you find work in Italy, you will be covered by the National Health Service (*Servizio Sanitario Nazionale*), which provides access to medical care and treatments. The National Pension Scheme provides retirement benefits based on eligibility criteria, such as contributions made throughout an individual's working years. You will pay income taxes and contribute to the Italian Social Security through payroll deductions. However, your employer will also make contributions on your behalf. Collective Bargaining Agreements (CBAs) between employers' associations and trade unions play a significant role in defining specific employment conditions and benefits in various industries and sectors.

Employees who cannot work due to illness or injury are entitled to Paid Sick Leave. The benefits associated with the duration of sick leave may depend on the length of your service and your work contract agreements. Female employees are entitled to Maternity Leave before and after childbirth, while mothers and fathers have access to Parental leave. Despite the ongoing efforts to promote diversity and inclusion in Italy, minorities may face barriers to accessing employment, a common challenge in many countries. Italian labor laws protect against unfair dismissal and workplace discrimination, allowing employees to challenge firings and seek compensation in case of discriminatory terminations. However, remember that everyone's situation is different, and if you find work in Italy, you should not let that deter you from pursuing your dream. As for the self-employed or retiree, this should not be an issue.

ITALY WORK VISA

Visto Per Lavoro In Italia

The Italy Work Visa is for people with a job offer or employment contract in Italy. It is granted for specific employment purposes and allows holders to work and reside legally in Italy. Depending on the duration of your employment in Italy, your visa might be a Short Stay Work Visa or a Long-Stay Work Visa. As the process is administered regionally, the requirements may vary slightly depending on the applicant's professional field. For instance, the Cultural or Sports Activities Visa requirements will probably differ from the Long Stay Skilled Work Visa.

There are two steps involved in obtaining a Work Visa in Italy. The employer is responsible for initiating the visa process on behalf of the employee. Firstly, they need to get clearance from the Employment Office (*Ufficio Provinciale del Lavoro e della Massima Occupazione*) by providing evidence that the employee, who is a non-resident foreigner, is qualified for the position and that the job is not suitable for an Italian national. Once the clearance is obtained or it is proven that there are no suitable Italian or EU candidates available for the job position, the employer can then proceed with the visa process by obtaining a Work Permit (*Nulla Osta*) on behalf of the applicant or employee from the local labor authorities or the Central Police Office or Police Headquarters (*Questura*).

> **Note**: The employee will provide all the necessary documentation to the employer before submission.

If approved, the employer, not the employee, will receive the Work Permit. Subsequently, the local authorities that issued the Work Permit will notify the employee's local Italian embassy or consulate about the approval, letting the embassy know they can issue the employee their Entry Visa. The consulate or embassy will then contact the employee via phone or email to inform them that the visa is ready for collection. The employee will have six months to collect the visa before traveling to Italy. Once in Italy, the employee must apply for a Residence Permit at the

Police Headquarters by submitting their Entry Visa and Work Permit.

> **Note**: The difference between an Entry Visa and a Work Permit is that the visa gives you the right to enter Italy, while the permit allows you to work in Italy.

Suppose you are already in Italy with a Self-employment visa and receive a job offer. In that case, you must go through the same process mentioned above, as you are applying for a different visa category. Your employer will initiate the process, and you must collect your visa from an Italian embassy or consulate outside of Italy.

WHAT YOU NEED FOR AN ITALY WORK VISA:

- A Job offer or work contract from an Italian employer
- A Work Permit/Authorization from the Italian government
- A passport (at least valid six months beyond the intended period of stay in Italy)
- Completed visa application forms
- Recent passport pictures
- Proof of accommodation in Italy, such as a rental contract or a letter from your host
- Proof of financial means (sufficient funds to support yourself and your family during your stay

in Italy, especially if you haven't secured accommodation or started working yet)

- ☞ Health insurance for the duration of your stay in Italy
- ☞ Certificate of "No Criminal Convictions" or a clean criminal record
- ☞ Medical examination, if applicable

HOW TO START A BUSINESS IN ITALY
Come Avviare Un'attività In Italia

Italy offers opportunities for entrepreneurs in various sectors, including tourism, fashion, design, food and beverage, and technology. The country also has a robust domestic market, a skilled workforce, and a rich cultural heritage that can contribute to business success.

However, even though the government has simplified administrative procedures and reduced bureaucracy, some processes are still time-consuming and require multiple steps, such as obtaining permits, registering with various authorities, and complying with regulations, since Italy has laws and regulations governing numerous business operations, including labor laws, taxation, licensing, and intellectual property rights. Understanding and complying with these legal requirements can be complex, particularly for foreign entrepreneurs unfamiliar with the Italian legal system. Requesting the help of local business organizations or advisors to navigate any legal or administrative procedures can be beneficial.

Remember that Italian is the primary language used in business and administration. This is Italy, after all. A good grasp of the language can facilitate communication and help navigate local business, practices, and customs. Understanding Italian business culture and building relationships with local partners and suppliers can also be advantageous.

Note: If you are counting on bank loans, grants, and venture capital, bear in mind that new or small businesses face even more significant challenges in accessing financing and funding.

If you are considering starting a business in Italy, finding a unique niche that appeals to the local market and sets you apart from the competition is crucial. Try to identify a demand that still needs to be met. I know a couple who moved to a new country to start an Airbnb business. They sold all their belongings to get new furniture once they had settled. Unbeknown to them, there were no furniture stores in their new city. The husband saw an opportunity and began making custom-made furniture by sourcing materials from an out-of-town supplier. The wife realized no restaurants offered healthy options and opened a small coffee shop that later became a full restaurant. Fortunately, they never started their Airbnb business, as they would have been just another fish in the pond. So, before starting a business, do your research and gain a good understanding of the market you're entering. Don't just pick an idea and go with it. Take the time to investigate the demand for your product or service and try to identify any competitors you may have. This way, you can be sure you're offering something unique that will appeal to your target market. And if you can, do something you love because, once again, there is no better reward than making a living out of your passion.

> **Note**: A professional will help you determine which documents you need for your type of business.

WHAT YOU NEED TO START A BUSINESS IN ITALY:

- Valid passport or ID card for all business owners, partners, and shareholders
- Proof of residence
- Company name, if applicable
- Articles of Association or Bylaws outlining your company's internal regulations and governance
- For specific legal structures, such as a Limited Liability Company (LLC), "*Società a Responsabilità Limitata,*" or simply "SRL," you must provide a Certificate of Incorporation, "*Atto Costitutivo* or *Atto di Costituzione,*" (obtained during the Italian Chamber of Commerce registration process)
- A Shareholders' Agreement (if there are multiple shareholders or partners in your business)
- A Business Tax Identification Number or "*Partita IVA*" (can be obtained from the Italian Revenue Agency, "*Agenzia delle Entrate,*" for small business owners or self-employed)

- ☞ Proof of funds such as bank statements or investment certificates
- ☞ Lease agreement or property ownership documents (if you rent or purchase a property for your business operations)
- ☞ Specific permits or licenses for regulated professions, such as food and health services
- ☞ General Liability Insurance or Professional Liability Insurance

Vernazza, Italy

HIRING A STAFF IN ITALY

Assumere Personale In Italia

Finding the right employees is one of the most important aspects for a business to succeed. The easy part is that Italians are great employees who take pride in their job performance. However, hiring staff in Italy comes with specific requirements, like an employment contract. Guaranteeing that the contract complies with Italian labor laws and includes the necessary clauses is essential. The country also has comprehensive labor laws that cover various aspects of employment, including minimum wages, working hours, overtime, paid leave, severance pay, and employee rights.

As an employer, you will be responsible for making social security contributions for your employees. Remember that Italian employees are entitled to paid vacation leave, typically ranging from 4 to 6 weeks per year, depending on the length of service, and that various sectors and industries in Italy have CBAs (Collective Bargaining Agreements) negotiated between employers' associations and trade unions. Depending on your industry, you may need to adhere to the relevant CBA.

Italy has a progressive income tax system, and you must calculate and withhold income tax from employee salaries. Expected employer benefits in Italy may include health insurance, pension plans, meal vouchers, and transportation allowances. Employees in Italy have various rights and protections, including protection against discrimination, harassment, and unfair treatment. Ending an employment relationship in Italy must be justified by valid reasons, as employees are entitled to notice periods or severance pay based on their length of service. You may require the services of an accountant familiar with Italian laws and regulations.

RENTING A SPACE FOR YOUR BUSINESS IN ITALY

Affittare Uno Spazio Per La Vostra Attività In Italia

Unless you work from home or share a workspace, you might need to rent one in Italy, with specific regulations and zoning laws dictating where businesses can operate. Large cities, such as Rome, Milan, and Florence, often experience high demand for commercial properties, making it more challenging to find available spaces. In contrast, smaller towns or less populated areas may have more readily available options, though it will depend on the type of business you run, whether online or in person. Additionally, the availability and competition of office spaces, retail storefronts, and industrial properties may vary. Working with a commercial real estate agent can simplify the search and negotiation process.

REGISTERING A FOREIGN COMPANY IN ITALY

Registrazione Di Una Società Straniera In Italia

Opening a branch of your business in Italy allows you to establish a presence in the country without creating a separate legal entity. However, before doing so, you must confirm that your company meets the eligibility criteria for establishing a branch in Italy. Typically, most types of businesses, including foreign corporations, are eligible. You will also need to appoint a legal representative based in Italy who will represent the branch in the country. This representative can be an individual or another legal entity. To register the branch, you must file the necessary paperwork with the National Business Register (*Registro delle Imprese*), managed by the Italian Chamber of Commerce (*Camera di Commercio*). You will need to provide various documents, including:

- ☞ A Certificate of Incorporation of your foreign company, the branch's bylaws, and details about the legal representative
- ☞ An Italian Tax Identification Number
- ☞ An Italian bank account in the branch's name

Like other businesses in Italy, branches are typically required to submit annual financial statements.

ITALY START-UP VISA (ISV)

Visto Lavoro Autonomo Start Up

Now, **suppose you have a solid business plan or a qualifying innovative start-up project**, enough funds in your bank account to support yourself until your business becomes profitable, or an endorsement from an Italian incubator, accelerator, or venture capital fund authorized by the Italian government to endorse start-up visa applications. In that case, you can apply anytime online for an Italy Start-up Visa for non-EU entrepreneurs and innovators. You don't need to be in Italy to apply for this visa unless you already live there and need to extend your stay. To qualify, a start-up must be under five years old, have a certain level of innovation in its products or services, and meet specific revenue and employee thresholds.

WHAT TYPE OF BUSINESS QUALIFIES FOR A START-UP VISA:

- ☞ Must be a limited company, "Ltd." or "SRL" (*Società a responsabilità limitata*) meaning it offers limited liability to its owners or shareholders

- ☞ Should not be listed on a regulated market or multilateral trading system

- ☞ Annual sales should not exceed 5 million euros

- ☞ Should not distribute dividends

- ☞ Must be engaged solely or primarily in technological innovation and should not have been created from a corporate merger or division

You can start by emailing the Italy Start-up Visa (ISV) Committee *atitaliastartupvisa@mise.gov.it*. You can also apply via Direct Application or Certified Incubator (if you already have their support) through. *https://italiastartupvisa.mise.gov.it/#Why_Italy* Certified incubators are companies that host startups by providing them with a space where they can develop their business. They also support business ideas by providing technical, legal, and management support and the necessary equipment to run their business.

You will need the following:

- ☞ Application form for ISV

- ☞ Presentation deck (.ppt format)

- ☞ Business plan with a forecast of costs and revenues
- ☞ Cover letter with financial statements
- ☞ Copy of passport

Once you have submitted your application, the Italian authorities will assess the business plan through a Technical Committee to ensure your business can generate income and contribute positively to the Italian economy. If the project is approved, they will issue a Letter of Endorsement, which can increase a startup's credibility when applying for other programs or funding opportunities. You will also get an Innovative Startup Certification, which provides official recognition to qualifying startups from the Italian Ministry of Economic Development, allowing you to apply for the Start-up Visa at your local Italian consulate or embassy. The certification has various benefits, including reduced taxation, exemptions, and access to government grants and funding opportunities.

The Start-up Visa allows the applicant to enter Italy and apply for a renewable Residence Permit for Start-up Entrepreneurs (*Permesso di Soggiorno per Intraprendenti*) at the local Police Station eight days after arrival. You will get permanent residence in Italy after five years. The Start-up Visa also allows family members (spouses and minor children) to apply for a Family Reunification Visa, granted for the duration specified in the application. However, if you already live in Italy and hold a valid Residence or Long-term Permit from another EU country, you can convert it to a start-up without leaving the country. To help you determine if a Start-up visa is the right choice, consult with legal and business professionals specializing in start-ups in Italy.

> **Note**: Those intending to join an existing start-up can also obtain the ISV.

WHAT YOU NEED FOR AN ITALIAN START-UP VISA:

- Visa application forms
- An ISV *"Nulla Osta"* or one backed by an incubator
- The Innovative Startup Certification delivered by the Italian Ministry of Economic Development (MISE)
- Sufficient financial resources like bank statements, evidence of investment, income tax returns, or other financial documents
- A valid passport with at least six months of validity beyond your intended stay in Italy
- Proof of health insurance
- Criminal record certificate, if applicable
- Proof of accommodation in Italy
- Proof of residence in your home country if applying outside of Italy
- Passport pictures
- Additional documents

REGISTERING YOUR BRAND IN ITALY
Registrazione Del Marchio In Italia

Trademark registration is optional in Italy, as extensive prior use is supposed to be sufficient to maintain trademark rights. Registration, however, will help enforce the trademark by granting the presumption of ownership. Once you can confirm the availability of your brand name in Italy, you can proceed with filing a trademark application with the Italian Patent and Trademark Office, UIBM (*Ufficio Italiano Brevetti e Marchi*). The application can be submitted online or in person. The UIBM will review your trademark application to ensure compliance with Italy's legal requirements. If granted, your brand protection will typically last for ten years, renewable for subsequent ten-year periods.

> **Note**: Consult the official website of the UIBM https://uibm.mise.gov.it/index.php/en for more detailed guidelines about registering your brand in Italy.

THE EU-BLUE CARD

The European Union Blue Card doubles as a Work Visa and Residency Permit for Highly Qualified Workers from non-EU countries who wish to live and work in an EU member state. The number of eligible people is relatively small, but preferences are given to business consultants,

doctors, engineers, professors, programmers, developers, managers, scientists, analysts, nurses, architects, and so on. The permit is valid for one to four years and allows applicants to work in 25 of the 27 EU member states except for Denmark and Ireland. The main benefit of the EU Blue Card is that once you have it, you won't need to go through the whole visa application again if you find work in the Schengen area, making it much easier to switch jobs; you must have worked for the same employer two consecutive years. It also gives the holder access to unemployment benefits for three months, a period during which you should be looking for another job, and guarantees other rights, such as family reunification, that some national work permits may not offer.

To be eligible for an EU Blue Card, your country of residence should not be in any of the Schengen member states. As the applicant, you'll need to gather necessary documents such as your passport, educational certificates, proof of accommodation, and any other documents required by the Italian authorities. Most importantly, you must have a work contract or a job offer in Italy. The job description should be in a high-skilled profession that aligns with your qualifications. Otherwise, you might run the risk of seeing your application denied. And your salary must meet the minimum threshold required for EU Blue Card holders in Italy. The application process may take up to 3 months, and your employer, the sponsor, will initiate the process by applying for the residence permit on your behalf by submitting the documents to the local immigration authorities in Italy, including the employment contract, proof of your qualifications, and evidence of efforts to recruit within the EU, meaning evidence that they have conducted a Labor Market Test to demonstrate that there were no suitable candidates from

Italy or the EU available for the position. You will apply for the Blue Card at the Italian consulate or embassy in your home country or your country of legal residence once your employer's application is approved (the immigration office in Italy will let the consulate know that your application has been approved). You may provide biometric data (fingerprints, photographs) and attend an interview at the consulate or embassy on the day of your appointment. If your application is approved, you'll receive your Blue Card and will be free to travel to Italy and start work.

> **Note**: Continuous legal residence and compliance with integration requirements can lead to permanent residency.

WHAT YOU NEED TO APPLY FOR AN EU-BLUE CARD:

- A valid passport
- Proof of your higher education degree or equivalent qualifications
- Job offer or employment contract from an Italian employer (should specify your job title, job description, salary, and duration of the contract)
- Labor Market Test
- Proof of valid health insurance (must cover both medical treatment and repatriation for the entire duration of your intended stay in Italy)
- Completed application forms
- Recent passport pictures

- ☞ Proof of accommodation, such as a rental contract or a letter from your host
- ☞ Clean criminal record, if applicable (will depend on the region)
- ☞ A detailed CV or resume
- ☞ Demonstrate language proficiency in Italian, if applicable
- ☞ Any other supporting documents, if applicable

Porticos, Florence, Italy

STUDYING IN ITALY
STUDIARE IN ITALIA

Adults considering studying in Italy and parents moving with children probably wonder, "How does Italy's education system work?" The good news is that Italy offers an array of public and private schools and universities, so finding a good school or college won't be difficult if you can narrow down your preferences and goals. Except for some international schools, private and public school programs usually follow the regulations set by the Ministry of Education, University and Research or "MIUR" (*Ministero dell'Istruzione, Università e Ricerca*).

For parents with young children, your choice of a daycare center or preschool will depend on your preferences and the availability of early childhood education services in the local area. As you can imagine, you will have more options in a big city than a small village. There may also be regional differences in the age at which children start preschool.

Daycare centers – *Asilo Nido* – cater to infants and young children from a few months to around three years old. They provide a nurturing environment and educational activities for babies and toddlers. They are not mandatory, hence not free, so attendance is optional, except for children with working parents. You should contact your city hall or "*Municipio*" to learn about their acceptance guidelines.

Kindergartens or preschools – *Scuola Dell'infanzia Comunale* – are managed by local municipalities and follow the national curriculum. They offer various activities for children between the ages of 3 and 6. Although attendance is not mandatory, parents recognize the program's benefits in developing children's social and cognitive skills before they start primary school. As they are free programs, the demand is high, and priority is given to municipality residents. If your child has special needs, inclusive preschools

(*Scuola dell'Infanzia Integrata*) have an excellent program for all the children involved. They provide education and support for children with special needs alongside their non-special needs peers.

Semi-private preschools – *Scuola dell'Infanzia Paritaria* – adhere to the national curriculum since they receive partial funding from the government. They are usually affordable and best if your goal is to transition to the public system. On the other hand, "*Scuola dell'Infanzia Privata*" is a fully private, independently operated preschool. It is best to look into each because they follow their own curriculum or guidelines.

International preschools – *Scuola dell'Infanzia Internazionale* – usually offer an international curriculum or bilingual programs, which means they might follow educational methods from other countries and focus on teaching different languages. You might already be familiar with Montessori schools (*Scuola dell'Infanzia Montessori*), which follow the educational approach developed by Maria Montessori by emphasizing individualized learning, hands-on activities, and independence. In contrast, the Reggio-Emilia approach (*Scuola di Reggio Emilia*), an educational philosophy developed in the city of Reggio Emilia in northern Italy, places the child at the center of the learning process through collaboration, group involvement, and the use of the environment as a tool for education and exploration. There are also preschools affiliated with religious institutions (*Scuola dell'Infanzia Religiosa*) that offer faith-based education along with the regular curriculum.

ITALIAN EDUCATION SYSTEM
Sistema Educativo Italiano

In Italy, children between 6 and 16 must attend school. However, for foreign children who barely speak the language, the experience could be very different from what they are used to. If your child will attend public school in Italy, it's a good idea to enroll them in a few Italian language courses. This will help them adjust better, make friends faster, and overall make the most out of their academic experience. The other option would be homeschooling.

Primary or Elementary School – *Scuola Primaria* – is attended by children aged 6 to 11 and consists of five grades. It is required for all Italian children. During this period, students learn basic subjects such as the Italian language, mathematics, science, history, geography, and foreign languages, with the study of religion being optional.

Middle School or Lower Secondary Education – *Scuola Secondaria Di Primo Grado* – lasts three years for students aged 11 to 13 who follow a comprehensive curriculum that includes core subjects as well as electives, culminating with an exam at the end of eighth grade (*Terza Meza.*)

High School or Upper Secondary Education – *Scuola Secondaria Di Secondo Grado* – lasts five years and involves students aged 14 to 19, even if school is mandatory till 16. Every high schooler is expected to take the final state exam (*Esame di Stato*)/(*Diploma de Maturità*) if they want the high school diploma.

> **Note**: In Italy, based on a student's academic performance, progress, and overall readiness for the next grade level, the school administration and teachers might decide to hold them back or make them repeat a grade.

Students can choose from 3 types of high schools based on their goals:

- Regular high school – *Liceo* – offers a more theoretical education classical. Students choose to major in different academic areas, such as classical, scientific, linguistic, and art studies.

- Technical-professional institute – *Istituto Tecnico* – focuses on technical and vocational education. It's best suited for those who want immediate insertion into the corporate world in technology, healthcare professions, etc.

☞ Professional institutes – *Istituti Professionali* – also offer vocational education and training that prepare students for specific professions. They are typically attended by students aged 14 to 19 after middle school. Graduates of an "*Istituto Professionale*" can pursue careers in mechanics, electronics, health services, graphic design, and more, or they can choose to continue their education through IFTS programs (*Istruzione e Formazione Tecnica Superiore*), which provide further vocational training.

Vocational Education and Training – *Istruzione E Formazione Tecnica Superiore* – or IFTS programs align with the concept of trade schools, where students gain practical skills in a specific trade or field, like plumber, electrician, hairdresser, beautician, etc. The goal is usually to bridge the gap between education and the demands of the job market by preparing students with hands-on experience directly relevant to specific professions or industries. IFTS students are usually job-ready once they have completed the program.

HOMESCHOOL IN ITALY
Educazione Domestica/ Istruzione Parentale

Homeschooling in Italy is legal and regulated by the government. However, there are specific requirements and procedures that parents must follow. They should first check with local education authorities for specific requirements and provide a Declaration of Intent to homeschool. The Declaration will include a program of study that should cover the subjects required by law, including Italian language, mathematics, science, history, and physical education. They should also include a list of educational resources and a schedule of activities. Depending on the region, children may be required to participate in extracurricular activities or social events to address concerns about socialization for homeschooled children. The Declaration should be updated annually and report on the child's progress, who might also be required to take some exams to assess their progress. Sometimes, local educational authorities may appoint a supervisory body to monitor homeschooling families to ensure academic standards are met. This is because some universities require standardized test scores or alternative assessments upon enrollment for homeschoolers.

UNIVERSITIES IN ITALY

Università In Italia

Higher education in Italy is highly regarded, with the country being home to some of the world's oldest and most prestigious universities. Given that Italian universities are well-regarded internationally, they attract many foreign students eager to participate in their Erasmus program, which facilitates student exchanges across European universities and international students looking for affordable education since Italy's public university tuition fees tend to be low.

However, you need a high school diploma to access the university in Italy. If your high school diploma is from a different country, have it translated and notarized in case you need it to apply for a visa or the university of your choice. While Italian is the primary language of instruction, some universities offer programs in English, especially at the graduate level, meaning you won't necessarily need to be fluent in Italian to pursue higher education in Italy. However, it might help in daily interactions with the staff or others. However, it would be best to contact your chosen university to learn about their language requirements.

The admission processes will vary based on the university and program. Some programs may require entrance exams, while others may have specific academic requirements. You must contact the university of your choice directly to learn more about the application process. Italy has several types of universities: traditional (*Uuniversità*), technical (*Politecnici*), and specialized institutions that offer a wide range of academic disciplines through three main degrees: Bachelor's (*Laurea*), Master's (*Laurea Magistrale*) or specialized degrees, that last 2 or 3 year, depending. Degrees such as law, pharmaceutical, engineering, and medicine are called "single-cycle degree courses." Ph.D. (*Dottorato di Ricerca*) is suitable for those who want to build a career in the academic world or work in research.

> **Note**: UK citizens are considered third-country nationals when it comes to studying in Italy. Depending on the length of your stay and other factors, you might need to apply for a Student Visa or just a Residency Permit. Your UK diplomas should be recognized in Italy, but since each university has its own admission process, you should contact them directly.

TOP ITALIAN UNIVERSITIES

The University of Bologna (*Università di Bologna*), founded in 1088, is one of the oldest universities in the world. Renowned for its history, it offers a wide variety of programs. The University of Milan (*Università degli Studi di Milano*) is known for its focus on research and provides a wide range of programs across different disciplines. At the same time, Bocconi University (*Università Bocconi*) is a costly private university in Milan specializing in economics, business, and law. "*Politecnico di Milano*" is a technical university specializing in engineering, architecture, and design and is highly regarded in Italy and internationally. The Sapienza University of Rome (*Università di Roma La Sapienza*) is one of Europe's largest and oldest universities. The University of Padua (*Università degli Studi di Padova*) was founded in 1222 in northern Italy, making it one of the world's oldest universities. The University of Florence (*Università degli Studi di Firenze*) is in the historic city of Florence and is mainly known for its humanities and arts departments. The "*Scuola Normale Superiore di Pisa*" – a very prestigious and highly selective institution that offers advanced education and research in various disciplines – and the University of Pisa (*Università di Pisa*), which has a solid academic reputation, are both in Pisa. Another university known for scientific research is the University of Turin (*Università degli Studi di Torino*).

ITALY STUDENT VISA

Visto Studenti

Before applying for a student visa, you must be accepted into a recognized educational institution in Italy, a university, college, or other educational program. Check the specific visa requirements through the official website of the Italian consulate or embassy in your country since they can vary based on your nationality and the program you intend to enroll in.

To apply, you will need to fill out a visa application form and provide necessary documents, which may include:

- Valid passport or travel document
- Acceptance letter from an Italian institution or university
- Proof of financial means to cover your expenses during your stay in Italy
- Health insurance coverage
- Passport pictures
- Application fees
- Proof of accommodation in Italy
- Proof of no criminal record
- Any additional documents required by the consulate

In some cases, you might be required to provide biometric data (fingerprints and pictures) at the consulate or embassy, and depending on your country and circumstances, you might also need to attend an interview. The processing time for student visas varies, so you should apply well before your intended travel date and, most importantly, before school starts because you want to be present for the first day of school, if not the first week. Once your visa application is processed, you'll receive a decision on whether your demand is approved or denied. If it is approved, you will be able to travel to Italy within the validity period of the visa, and they will explain in case you need to apply for a Residence Permit upon arrival in Italy, which, once more, will depend on the length of stay and country of origin.

> **Note**: Foreign nationals holding a valid Italy Residence Permit for study, internship, or training can convert the permit into an Italian Work Permit without being subject to a quota.

Students from non-European Union (EU) countries studying in Italy with a valid Student Residence Permit can work part-time up to 20 hours per week during the academic year and full-time during school breaks. The permit contains information about the student's right to work and the number of hours permitted. Students may work in various types of employment, including internships, part-time jobs, and temporary positions, but some types of work, such as self-employment, may be restricted. After completing their studies, students can convert their student work permit into a regular work permit by getting a steady job or starting their own business. Some universities and institutions in Italy also provide employment assistance services to help students find work opportunities.

PROS OF STUDYING IN ITALY
Vantaggi Dello Studiare

- ☞ Students can immerse themselves in a country with a deep cultural heritage, exploring historical sites, museums, and vibrant traditions, with the culinary experience adding to the overall cultural immersion.

- ☞ Italy's central location in Europe makes it a convenient base for traveling to other European countries. Studying there can open doors to various career opportunities such as fashion, design, automotive, etc.

- ☞ Italy is home to several prestigious universities that attract students worldwide, offering various fields of study and interdisciplinary programs.

- ☞ Compared to some other Western European countries, Italy offers relatively affordable tuition fees for international students. The cost of living can vary, but it is considered reasonable in many regions.

- ☞ Students with families can have their spouses and children join them if they have a valid Italian Student Permit.

CONS OF STUDYING IN ITALY
Svantaggi Dello Studiare

- ☞ While many universities offer programs in English, particularly at the master's and doctoral levels, there might still be a language barrier for students who are not fluent in Italian, and finding employment may be challenging for the same reasons.

- ☞ Italy is known for its bureaucratic processes, and students may encounter challenges when dealing with administrative tasks, visa applications, and residence permits.

- ☞ The cost of living in some major Italian cities, particularly in the north, can be relatively high. Accommodation, transportation, and daily expenses may be challenging for students on a budget.

- ☞ Some areas in Italy may face challenges with infrastructure and public services. Issues like public transportation reliability, occasional strikes, and variations in service quality may affect the overall student experience.

- ☞ In certain regions and smaller towns, English may be less widely spoken in daily life compared to larger cities and tourist areas. This can make communication and socializing more challenging for international students.

Cisternino, Italy

RETIRING IN ITALY

PENSIONE IN ITALIA

Italy is a great place to live and a great retirement destination due to its rich culture, history, cuisine, weather, and beautiful landscapes. But contrary to other countries, Italy doesn't have a Golden Visa. Most people who retire in Italy tend to do so by applying for an Elective visa, meaning they are self-sufficient and won't need a job in Italy. However, like anywhere else, whoever chooses to spend their retirement in Italy should consider the lifestyle they want, their values and priorities, and plan accordingly. I know a woman who moved to Costa Rica. Although she had never visited the country, she knew she wanted to live in a warm climate. After living there for a year, she decided to make it her permanent home. She chose a location near the mountains for the peacefulness and built a house on top of a hill. Besides grazing cows, she had no immediate neighbors, which was ideal for her. However, she soon discovered that during the rainy seasons, the cold was making her arthritis worse. Moreover, her car would get stuck in the mud, and she would have to get out and walk up the hill in the rain. This emphasizes the importance of considering long-term factors when choosing a location. If you are considering living in a small Italian village, carefully examine the transportation system, especially if you have mobility issues. Additionally, it is important to know that cobblestone streets can be dangerous and require extra caution. Other factors to consider when making your decision include the proximity of hospitals and airports, the availability of grocery stores (there are not many options for ethnic foods in smaller towns), cultural events and social clubs, and the overall cost of living in the area.

Remember that buying property in Italy won't give you access to a visa. Though the costs of living will vary according to region, this beautiful country can be an expensive place to live in, particularly in major cities like Rome, Milan, and Venice. Therefore, even if Italy remains more affordable than most Western countries, it's crucial to have a stable source of income to cover all your living expenses. Some retirees spend half a year in Italy and the other half in their countries either for tax purposes, health issues, or to remain close to their families. Consult with tax experts specializing in international retirement to understand Italy's tax laws and any international agreements that may affect your financial situation.

Italy has a high-quality healthcare system, but it's essential to understand how it works, especially if you're not an EU citizen. Several governmental benefits exist for people over 60 with limited income who can access the health system at no cost. However, depending on your age and overall health, you may need to get private health insurance in addition to the national healthcare system. If you are considering moving to Italy but don't know yet if it will be suitable for you, take advantage of the Schengen tourist visa and spend three months in the town or village you want to retire in, living a regular life, doing what you would be doing if you were to live there. Go during summer to see how touristy the place can get. Or, if you have never experienced winter and plan to settle in the North, go during the coldest month. Once you have decided that "the grass is indeed greener on the other side," go back home, pack everything, and go embrace *"la dolce vita."*

WHY RETIRE IN ITALY

Perchè Andare In Pensione In Italia

If you have decided to retire in Italy, that's probably because you long for a healthier and wealthier life. Whether you adopt the Mediterranean or the Blue Zone diet, you will enjoy an outstanding quality of everyday life in Italy. You will experience "from farm to table food," meaning no processed food, especially if you stay in a small village, which will also lower your cost of living. Being a peninsula, Italy has many beaches, mountains, rolling hills, and a diverse climate. Regardless of where you live, the food is exceptional, with each region having unique culinary specialties. You will have access to the Schengen area, which means you can easily travel to other parts of Europe and the world. You will have the opportunity to learn about a new culture and language and, hopefully, make new friends, which you can do by visiting the city hall and asking about joining existing clubs or creating your own.

"CONS" OF RETIRING IN ITALY
Svantaggi Del Pensionamento In Italia

Besides getting accustomed to the different types of visas and the Italian tax system, the language barrier will probably be the hardest challenge if you don't already know Italian. If you live in a small town, you also won't have a lot of culinary choices besides Italian food, so no more Mexican or Indian food. It might be hard to make new friends if you live in a small village with few social gatherings, or worse, you might find yourself stuck in a lifestyle that doesn't fit your vision of retirement or Italy. The upside of retirement is that you can choose where and how to live your retirement years. If you dream of living a quiet but culturally rich life, waking up to stunning views, eating the best food, and traveling throughout Europe, then Italy is the right place.

ITALY ELECTIVE RESIDENCY VISA (TYPE D VISA)
Visto Residenza Elettiva

The Italy Elective Residence Visa (ERV) **is** a type of Long-Stay Visa designed **for foreign nationals who wish to live in Italy for over a year and have the financial means to support themselves without working**. Often referred to as **Italy Retirement Visa**, it is mainly used by foreign nationals or anyone who is not from an EU country, Switzerland, Norway, Iceland, or Lichtenstein, and who wishes to live permanently in Italy for non-work-related reasons.

> **Note:** The Italian Elective Visa does not allow you to work or seek employment under any conditions. You will need to switch to a Work Visa if you decide to come out of retirement.

The application process for an Elective Residence Visa can vary depending on the Italian consulate or embassy in your home country. You must follow their specific instructions and provide all the required documents, meaning you will need to make copies of all your documents and bring them with you on the day of your appointment. If you can afford an Italian immigration lawyer, do so. They will advise on the type of visa to get; all you have to do is handle the documents, and they will take care of all the paperwork for you. The processing time for an Elective visa application may be up to ninety days and cannot be accelerated. This visa is the most strictly regulated, and consular officers tend to examine the applications meticulously and may request additional documents. Therefore, you should submit your visa request at least ninety days before your expected departure date and avoid buying airplane tickets before you get your visa in case of a rejection. There might not be a strict language requirement for the Elective Residence Visa. Still, a basic understanding of Italian can benefit daily interactions and integration into the local community.

> **Note:** Submitting all required documentation does not automatically guarantee that you will get the visa, but it will save you time.

Before you apply, know that your passport must be valid for at least three months beyond the validity date of the requested visa and must have two consecutive blank pages available for the visa. You should also be able to provide detailed documentation of your sources of income, such as social security, state or private company pensions, monthly payments generated by house/apartment rentals, bank statements with the amount of available funds, 401K statements if applicable, brokerage account statements, retirement accounts documents of business ownership and related documentation. The requirement for financial requirements will vary depending on factors such as family size and the cost of living where you intend to live (big city vs small town). If renting or leasing, be ready to show the original copy of a one-year signed rental agreement (*Contratto di Locazione ad Uso Abitativo*), with proof that their landlord has registered it with the Italian tax authorities. Or, if you own the property, a title of ownership with proof of registration with the Italian Tax Agency (*Agenzia delle Entrate*).

Keep in mind that the list below is a suggestion of documents you may be asked to provide since every embassy operates differently. If you think of any other documents that can help your case, have them ready. The more prepared you are, the less stressful the whole process will be.

WHAT YOU NEED FOR AN ITALIAN ELECTIVE RESIDENCE VISA:

- A valid passport and travel document.
- Proof of residence in your home country, such as driver's license, ID, water, gas, or electricity bill
- Completed and clearly filled out visa application forms for each applicant to be signed in the presence of a Consular Officer
- Two recent passport-size pictures
- A letter explaining the reason for travel, length of stay, place of residence, and names of persons accompanying the applicant
- Proof of financial means to support your stay in Italy without needing employment
- Health insurance coverage for you and your dependents for the validity of your stay in Italy
- Criminal record clearances or background check
- Proof of accommodation in Italy
- Certified copies of marriage and birth certificates, if applicable
- Visa fees
- Any other documents required by the Italian consulate or embassy, such as tax returns, self-addressed pre-paid envelopes, etc.

> **Note**: Airbnb, hotel reservations, and such cannot be accepted for this type of visa. The visa will be denied if the applicant does not have a lease, rental contract, or deed in their name.

The Elective Residency Visa is valid for exactly 365 days. This means you need to enter Italy within a year. As for any Long-stay Visa, applicants usually must apply for a Residence Permit at the local Police Headquarters, usually eight days after entering the country. The Permit will be renewed annually, allowing applicants to stay legally in Italy beyond the visa's initial duration.

Brescia, Italy

BUREAUCRACY IN ITALY

BUROCRAZIA IN ITALIA

The popular saying "there is no place like home" could also be applied to Italy because "there is no place like Italy," a fantastic and unique country, except for bureaucracy. Fortunately, this is not only the case for Italy. Every major country has a large bureaucratic system that can be efficient in some aspects and disastrous in others. Overall, Italians prefer to handle things in person instead of online, which leads to longer waiting times and frustration. Public services are said to be better in Central and Northern Italy, but ultimately, it depends on the person you are dealing with. When going to places like the Police Headquarters, it's best to bring a computer, phone (and charger), a magazine, a friend, or anything to keep you occupied while waiting. Some days, the process might be relatively quick, but you might find yourself impatiently tapping your foot on other days. Before heading anywhere, look online first. Check to see if what you need can be done remotely; if not, look for the proper administrative office, find the list of documents you need, and then make the appointment. Nevertheless, you will eventually get used to it unless you have a few hundred euros to spare and can pay someone to handle all the bureaucracy.

Italy Public Administration provides a **Public System for Digital Identity,** or SPID – a digital identity that includes a username and password – that enables Italian citizens and residents to access all government services: the National Institute for Social Security (INPS,) the National Revenue Agency *(Agenzia delle Entrate)*, the Ministry of Education, University, and Research (MIUR), the National Institute for Insurance Against Labor Accidents (INAIL) and the municipalities.

WHAT YOU NEED TO GET A SPID:

- Valid ID document (Residency Permit, Passport, or Driver's License)
- Health or tax card
- Personal email address
- Mobile phone number

INTEGRATION AGREEMENT
Accordo Di Integrazione

Foreigners over 16 who enter Italy and apply for a residence permit with a validity of at least one year are required to sign the 'Integration Agreement' at the Immigration Office or Police Headquarters. These agreements are part of Italy's efforts to promote the integration of immigrants into Italian society. They outline the rights and responsibilities of immigrants living in Italy and cover various aspects of integration, including language learning, cultural understanding, access to education and employment, and respect for Italian laws and values while also promoting diversity, tolerance, and mutual understanding.

REGISTER OF VITAL STATISTICS
Anagrafe

You will find them in each Town Hall (*Comune*). This is where all individuals living in the municipality jurisdiction must be registered.

POLICE HEADQUARTERS / POLICE CENTRAL OFFICE / MAIN POLICE STATION
Questura

In Italy, the Police Headquarters or Police Central Office is the primary authority responsible for most standard immigration procedures and various law enforcement and administrative tasks. The foreigner's office (*Ufficio Stranieri*) is the office competent for all immigration matters within the Police Office. They handle applications and renewals for residence permits, assist with visa applications, including long-stay visas, provide information and processing of work authorizations, and offer documentation for family members who wish to join their relatives in Italy. They also provide information about integration programs and services available to immigrants and offer basic legal information and guidance on immigration laws and regulations. Some offices also manage driving licenses and civil registry functions such as recording births, marriages, and deaths.

If you can, go there early in the morning to avoid waiting in line, which can still happen even if you have an appointment, and make sure you are getting the right ticket if you don't want to be sent back in line. Also, avoid going there during summer break because that's when Italian nationals who live abroad return home and need to renew or get their documents done since it is easier and less expensive to do it in Italy than at an Italian consulate or embassy. The services and duties provided by the Police Headquarters may differ from one province or region to another. If you intend to interact with a Police headquarters for issues related to immigration, residency, or any other matter, it is recommended to contact the specific office in the area where you live or plan to visit. This will guarantee that you receive the most precise information and support. Even though the Police Headquarter is responsible for immigration, sometimes you might have to deal with the administrative division or jurisdiction known as *"Prefecttura,"* instead. While the Police Headquarters operates locally, the "*Prefecttura*" is a regional administrative body representing the central government and can be involved in certain immigration-related matters.

IMMIGRATION OFFICE

Sportello Unico Per L'immigrazione

"Sportello Unico per l'Immigrazione" is an Italian term that means "One-Stop Shop for Immigration." This office, usually found at the "*Preffetura*," aims to simplify and centralize various immigration-related procedures and services for foreigners in Italy. The specific services provided by the Immigration Office can vary depending on the location and the policies of the local immigration office. Like the Police Headquarters, they may also help with

residence permits, visa applications, work authorizations, family reunification, and other immigration-related services.

> **Note**: The Immigration Office and the Police Headquarters are two distinct entities involved in immigration policies in Italy that play different roles within the overall immigration system. The Immigration Office is often associated with local immigration offices and may operate within or in coordination with the local Police Headquarters. While the "*Sportello Unico*" aims to simplify the process for individuals dealing with immigration matters, the "*Questura*" is a broader entity responsible for public security and immigration-related administrative tasks. When dealing with immigration matters, individuals may interact with both entities, depending on the specific services they require. It's advisable to contact the local immigration office for accurate and up-to-date information on procedures, requirements, and available services in your area.

CERTIFICATE OF NO IMPEDIMENT

WORK PERMIT/ENTRY PERMIT/CERTIFICATION/AUTHORIZATION/CLEARANCE/WAIVER

Nulla Osta

In Italy, a *"Nulla Osta"* (NOO-lah OH-stah) is commonly required in cases where the authorization or approval of the Italian authorities is needed, indicating that there are "no legal objections or obstructions" to a specific action or request. The application process may differ depending on the type of visa you are applying for. For instance, if you need one for business-related activities or self-employment, you may need to contact the local Chamber of Commerce where you plan to operate. If you are requesting one for employment, particularly if you have a job offer in Italy, your employer may need to initiate the process. If you are applying for a Study or Research Visa, you may obtain one from your home country's Italian consulate or embassy. In some cases, the academic institution or university may facilitate or initiate this process. For family reunification purposes, the family member in Italy typically needs to start the process by applying on behalf of the family member joining them. Start-up visa applicants may need to submit their request to the Italian consulate or embassy in their home country. The process may also involve one from Italian immigration authorities, such as MISE.

Here are cases where a *"Nulla Osta"* may be needed:

- Work Permit for Non-EU citizens (*Nulla Osta al Lavoro*)
- Marriage certificates to demonstrate that there are no legal obstructions to union
- Students from non-EU countries
- Non-EU citizens applying for a Residence Permit in Italy, in some cases
- Family reunification for non-EU family members of Italian citizens or non-EU residents with a valid Residence Permit
- Foreign artists, performers, or athletes planning to work or participate in events in Italy

☞ Foreign entrepreneurs or business owners who intend to establish or invest in Italy

> **Note**: You don't need a *"Nulla Osta"* for a Schengen Visa, and you won't need one once you become a citizen.

You can apply at an Immigration Office, the Police Headquarters, or your local Italian embassy if you are applying from your country. Applications submitted towards the end of each year are typically processed at the beginning of the following year. The list of required documents will depend on the type of authorization or clearance you are applying for. For example, someone looking for a marriage certificate must provide "a declaration of intent to marry," proof of civil status, and any divorce papers, if applicable, on top of the completed application forms, passport, and proof of residence. There are instances where you will have to pay processing fees, and depending on your country of origin, the documents submitted may need to be translated, legalized, or apostilled. The processing time is 90 days from the time of application, which might be less, depending on your request, with a six-month validity from the issue date. Although obtaining a *"Nulla Osta"* is the initial step to getting a visa, it does not guarantee visa approval.

SYNDICATES/ASSOCIATIONS/ NON-PROFITS
Patronati

If you are not fluent in Italian, can't afford a lawyer, or don't have an employer taking care of all your administrative processes, you can get help from a "*Patronate.*" Sometimes, the Post Office or the Police Headquarters will direct you to them; otherwise, ask where to find one. The Italian government recognizes these not-for-profit organizations whose primary role is to help people navigate complex administrative processes, such as applying for residence permits, social benefits, pensions, healthcare services, and other forms of government assistance. In a word, they help bridge the gap between citizens and government institutions, making the process more accessible and less intimidating. They offer free to low-cost services that can be beneficial for those who are unfamiliar with Italian bureaucratic procedures and legal complexities or face language barriers or other challenges.

Vatican City, Rome, Italy

ITALY RESIDENCE PERMIT

Permesso Di Soggiorno

The Italy Residence Permit or Permit of Stay is an official document allowing non-EU citizens to reside in Italy for an extended period, whether for work, study, family reunification, elective residence, or other reasons. It is granted by the Italian government and is essential for maintaining legal residency status in the country. The duration and the application process usually depend on the reason for your stay, which can range from a few months to several years.

Approximately eight days after you arrive in Italy with your entry visa, you will go to the "*Poste*" (Post Office) to request a "*Kit Postale*" for a Residency Permit. Look for post offices that say "*Sportello Amico,*" since not all post offices offer the service. The "*kit*" will contain all the application forms and a list of documents to provide. And that's where CAFs (Tax Assistant Centers), see below, and the Syndicates come in handy if you need help. If you have a lawyer or an employer, they will take care of everything. But if you don't and have a limited understanding of the Italian language, they will help you navigate the application process for a modest fee.

Once you have completed the application forms and made photocopies of all the required documents, you will return the "*kit*" to the Post Office or designated acceptance locations and pay all the fees. You won't pay anything at the Police Headquarters; all the fees will be paid at the Post Office. They will give you a receipt (*Ricevuta Postale*) and make the appointment with the local Police Station or relevant immigration office on your behalf. They will ask for your email or phone number to notify you of the day of your appointment with the immigration office. The appointments usually take place in the morning, and sometimes, they will give only a limited number of tickets; because of that, people get there as early as 6 a.m. to secure a ticket. Bring something to keep you warm and busy if you must get there early. Also, be prepared not to get everything sorted out the first time, especially if you don't speak Italian, because you might find out too late that no one in the entire immigration office speaks English. You will submit the originals and copies of all your required documents; they will also take your fingerprints (*Cattura degli Impronte Digitali* or *Impronte Digitali*), ask a few questions, and give you a receipt, which you should keep safely. It will serve as proof of residency until you get your real permit, which can take weeks. Suppose you need to apply for public services but still don't have your permit; you can always show the appointment receipt instead of the actual permit. You will be notified when the permit is ready.

Family members of Residence Permit holders may also be eligible to obtain their permits based on Family Reunification Visas. Possessing a valid Residence Permit often gives access to the Italian Healthcare System. If your situation changes, whether you switch jobs or move to a different city, you may need to update your Residence Permit accordingly. Finally, having a long-term Residence Permit may be a requirement for applying for Permanent Residency or Citizenship in Italy. Residence Permits are often renewable, usually every two years. You must start the renewal process before your current permit expires and follow the same steps as the first time.

WHAT YOU NEED FOR ITALY RESIDENCE PERMIT:

- ☞ Fill out the application form specific to the type of residence permit you are applying for
- ☞ Valid passport with at least six months of validity beyond your intended stay
- ☞ Recent passport-sized pictures
- ☞ Documents supporting the purpose of your stay in Italy (a job offer, acceptance letter from a school or university, proof of family reunification, etc.)
- ☞ Proof of residence in Italy
- ☞ Proof of sufficient financial means
- ☞ Proof of health insurance coverage
- ☞ Criminal record certificate or a police clearance certificate from the country you've lived in recently
- ☞ Medical examination, if applicable
- ☞ For family reunification, documents proving your relationship with your Italian relative
- ☞ Demonstrate a basic level of proficiency in the Italian language, if applicable
- ☞ For a work residence permit, you might need to provide additional documents from your employer
- ☞ Residence permit application processing fees

> **Note**: If your documents are not in Italian, you'll need to have them translated by an official translator and legalized or with apostilles.

TAX ASSISTANT CENTER

Centro Di Assistenza Fiscale (Caf)

Tax Assistant Centers (CAFs) are other nonprofit organizations that assist individuals, families, and businesses with various tax and administrative matters. Tax center services are precious for individuals who may need more understanding of the Italian tax and administrative systems, face language barriers, or need assistance due to specific circumstances. It's important to note that they operate independently and are not part of the government, although they are regulated by specific laws and regulations. Their services are typically offered to the public for free or at a low price. If you need assistance with tax-related matters or administrative procedures in Italy, contacting a tax center could be helpful. They can help fill out various forms and gather the documentation required for tax filings, benefit applications, and other administrative processes. For example, they can assist with preparing and submitting tax returns, guaranteeing that all necessary documents are in order and that the proper deductions and exemptions are applied.

They also provide guidance on accessing social security benefits, pensions, healthcare services, and other forms of government assistance, help understand eligibility criteria, and assist with the application process. Even though they are not law firms or financial institutions, they primarily focus on providing basic legal and financial information related to tax and administrative matters and various bureaucratic procedures, such as registering for social services, dealing with government agencies, and obtaining residency permits.

TAXES IN ITALY
Tasse In Italia

Tax regulations in Italy can be complex and subject to change. Suppose you plan to retire or be self-employed in Italy. In that case, it's better to get advice from tax professionals or the Italian tax authorities to make sure you follow current tax laws and regulations. Though Italy has high taxes, there are other European countries with higher tax rates. In case you qualify as a resident for tax purposes, Italy has a progressive income tax system (*Imposta sul Reddito delle Persone Fisiche*) or IRPEF, which can go up to 43%, depending on your income level. Add to that the regional surcharges that can vary by region. As a resident, you will also be expected to report your foreign income since Italy has tax treaties with many countries to avoid Double Taxation (being taxed on the same income in multiple countries). You should check whether your country has one with Italy to determine how your income will be taxed.

High-net-worth individuals and retirees usually choose the "Resident Non-Domiciled" regime, also known as the "Flat Tax Regime," a special tax regime available to individuals who become Italian tax residents but are not considered residents. If you are a non-resident, your tax liability in

Italy is typically limited to income earned within the country. You may be subject to the Non-Resident Taxation, which withholds tax at various rates depending on the type of income. Common sources of taxable income for non-residents may include employment income from working temporarily in Italy for foreign workers, rental income for property owners who do not reside in Italy, and individuals with income from Italian investments.

Italy also has a Wealth Tax (*Imposta sulle Grandi Fortune*) distinct from income taxes. It is typically calculated based on the total value of an individual's assets, including real estate, financial holdings, investments, jewelry, vehicles, and more. One of its primary purposes is to address economic inequality by taxing the accumulated wealth of the wealthiest members of society and using the revenue for public services or welfare programs. "Inheritance" and "Gift" taxes are applied when transferring assets between individuals. The rates and exemptions can vary based on the relationship between the donor and the recipient, something to remember if you choose to take Italian citizenship.

Property Tax, or IMU (*Imposta Municipale Propria*), is imposed on real estate properties and is calculated based on the property's value and local rates set by municipalities. So, before buying that charming old house that looks right out of a fairytale, ask about the property taxes first. Besides the fact that local municipalities in Italy can impose additional taxes or charges, such as the Municipal Tax, TASI (*Tassa Sui Servizi Indivisibili*), to finance public services, most goods and services are also subject to a consumption tax, IVA (*Imposta sul Valore Aggiunto*) or Value Added Tax (VAT).

Whether you work for or own a company, in both cases, you will be required to contribute to the Italian Social Security System (*Sistema di Sicurezza Sociale*). The contributions fund various social benefits, including healthcare, pensions, and unemployment benefits. Businesses or companies are subjected to a corporate tax rate. Furthermore, regional taxes and deductions can also impact the effective tax rate.

Getting professional tax advice from tax consultants or accountants with expertise in Italian taxation will guarantee that you comply with all relevant tax laws and make the most of any available tax benefits or credits. Additionally, tax treaties and rules may vary based on your country of origin, so it's essential to understand both Italian and international tax regulations that apply to your situation.

INDIVIDUAL TAX IDENTIFICATION NUMBER/TAX CODE
Codice Fiscale

Italian citizens are typically automatically assigned a Tax Identification Number at birth (*Codice Fiscale*), a unique 16-character code, including letters and numbers based on your personal information, such as your name, date of birth, and place of birth. It is a unique identifier for dealing with various administrative procedures and financial purposes, including opening bank accounts, signing employment contracts, filing taxes, financial transactions, official documentation, registering for utilities (electricity, water, etc.,), registering for healthcare services etc. The Italian tax number – similar to the USA Taxpayer Identification Number (TIN) or the UK National Insurance Number (NIN) – is issued by the local Italian tax office (*Agenzia delle Entrate*) or designated post offices. Getting one does not imply that you will have to pay taxes in Italy.

You will need to provide the following documents:

- Filled-out application forms
- Passport or ID
- Residence permit (for non-EU/EEA citizens)
- Proof of address
- Explain why you need a tax number (personal use, work-related, other purposes)
- Depending on your specific case (such as being a minor or having unique circumstances), you might need to provide additional documentation

After submitting the required documents and completing the application form, the authorities will process your request and issue you a tax number. You might get a physical card with your tax number on it, or you might get the code digitally. In some instances, temporary stay, tourists, EU/EEA citizens, and EHIC holders staying in Italy may also require one.

SELF-EMPLOYED TAX CODE / NUMBER

Partita Iva: Partita Individuale Di Identificazione Fiscale

This tax code is used for identifying individuals and entities engaged in economic activities, including self-employed professionals and businesses. It is basically a VAT (Value Added Tax) identification number. After registering your business with the Chamber of Commerce in the area where you plan to operate, you will register with the Italian Revenue Agency to get your Partita IVA. You must provide a list of documents, including personal identification, proof of residence, and details about your business activities. Depending on the nature of your business, you may have VAT obligations, with your Partita IVA serving as your VAT number.

Monopoli, Puglia, Italy

CURRENCY IN ITALY

Valuta In Italia

Like the rest of the EU, Italy uses the Euro (€) as its official currency. It is usually divided into coins and banknotes: coins are divided into 1 cent, 2 cents, 5 cents, 10 cents, 20 cents, 50 cents, €1, and €2. Banknotes come in the following forms: €5, €10, €20, €50, €100, €200, and €500. While credit and debit cards are widely accepted, cash is still commonly used in Italy for various transactions, especially in smaller establishments or local markets. Visa and Mastercard are the most accepted card networks, while American Express and other cards are accepted in only some places. However, a growing number of stores use contactless payment methods or mobile wallets (think Apple Pay or Google Pay).

> **Note**: Always have some cash on hand for smaller purchases.

There are no strict currency exchange controls for tourists visiting Italy but try to declare any significant sums of money when entering or leaving the country. Banks can also help you with currency exchange, especially for major currencies, so check with your bank first. Otherwise, you can do it at authorized currency exchange offices, banks, or ATMs in Italy. Since exchange rates and fees can vary, compare rates and read the terms before proceeding to the exchange. As stated earlier, prices in Italy generally include VAT (Value Added Tax), which is a consumption tax. If you're a non-EU resident, you might be eligible for a VAT refund on certain purchases made in Italy. Look for the "Tax-Free" or "Global Blue" signs in participating stores.

HERE ARE FEW USEFUL EXPRESSIONS:

- *"Soldi"*, *"Denaro"*: Money
- *"No hon contanti"*: I don't have any cash.
- *"Pagare"*: To pay
- *"Bancomat"*: ATM
- *"Contante"*: Cash
- *"Prelievo"*: Withdrawal
- *"Saldo"*: Balance
- *"Conto"*: Account
- *"Codice PIN"*: PIN
- *"Inserire la carta"*: Insert Card
- *"Inserire il PIN"*: Enter PIN
- *"Selezionare la lingua"*: Select Language
- *"Importo"*: Amount
- *"Ricevuta"*: Receipt
- *"Conferma"*: Confirm
- *"Annulla"*: Cancel
- *"Transazione"*: Transaction
- *"Attendere prego"*: Please Wait
- *"Carta trattenuta"*: Card Retained

☞ *"Fondi non disponibili"*: No Funds Available

☞ *"Hai bisogno di una ricevuta?"*: Do You Need a Receipt?

☞ *"Vuoi effettuare un'altra transazione?"*: Would You Like Another Transaction?

☞ *"Posso fare un bonifico bancario?"*: Can I make a bank transfer?

BANKING IN ITALY

Banche In Italia

Italy's banking system operates similarly to banking systems in other developed countries. The country has various types of banks: commercial, cooperative, savings, and foreign. Some well-known Italian banks include UniCredit, Intesa Sanpaolo, and Banco BPM. However, the Bank of Italy (*Banca d'Italia*) is Italy's central bank and financial regulator, overseeing the country's banking system and ensuring stability.

You can open different bank accounts in Italy, such as current or checking accounts (*Conto Corrente*) for day-to-day transactions, savings accounts (*Conto Risparmio*), and specialized accounts for specific purposes. Many Italian banks offer online banking platforms and mobile apps that allow you to conveniently manage your accounts, make transfers, pay bills, and access other banking services.

> **Note**: It's important to know the fees associated with your chosen bank and account type.

ATMs (Automated Teller Machines), commonly referred to as "*Bancomat*," which is a combination of the Italian words "*Banca*" (bank) and "*Automat*" (automated), are widespread throughout Italy, allowing you to withdraw cash using your debit or credit card. Check with your bank about any fees associated with international withdrawals. Also, remember that most modern ATMs in Italy offer language options, so you can often select English or another preferred language for your transactions. However, having a basic understanding of Italian terms can still be helpful, especially in areas where English may be less widely spoken.

Traditional banking hours in Italy are generally from Monday to Friday, around 8:30 AM to 4:00 PM. Remember that most businesses in Italy have a cultural practice that consists of closing for long lunch hours, even though, in recent years, some banks have chosen to remain open all day to accommodate different customer needs and working patterns in larger urban areas. Some banks might even open on Saturday mornings.

MONEY TRANSFER

Bonifico Bancario

Banks in Italy may charge fees for various services, including account maintenance, ATM withdrawals, and wire transfers. Transferring money to Italy can be done through various methods, depending on the amount, urgency, and convenience you need. Italian banks offer international money transfers and foreign currency accounts. Bank Wire Transfer is a direct transfer of funds from your local bank account to the recipient's bank account in Italy. You'll need the recipient's bank details, including IBAN (International Bank Account Number) and BIC/SWIFT code. Your bank will facilitate the transfer, and there might be fees involved, both from your bank and the recipient's bank.

Some mobile banking apps offer international money transfer services. Check with your bank if they provide this service. Otherwise, money transfer platforms like Wise, PayPal, or similar services allow you to send money internationally. These services often offer competitive exchange rates and lower fees than traditional banks. Unless you would rather write an international check, in which case try to remember that checks can take longer to clear, and fees may apply. Some people would transfer cash through money transfer companies like Western Union or MoneyGram. This method is suitable for urgent transfers but can be more expensive due to higher fees and less favorable exchange rates. A bank draft, also known as a cashier's check or banker's draft, is a secure way to transfer funds; you purchase a bank draft from your bank and send it to the recipient, who can deposit it into their bank account.

> **Note:** Some people use cryptocurrency to transfer money internationally. Bitcoin and other cryptocurrencies can be sent to recipients who have cryptocurrency wallets.

Remember that specific banking practices, services, and regulations vary among banks. So, research and compare different banks and their offers to find the best fit for your banking needs.

WHAT YOU NEED TO OPEN A BANK ACCOUNT IN ITALY:

- ☞ Tax identification number (*Codice Fiscale*)
- ☞ Identification documents such as a passport, driver's license, or ID card
- ☞ Proof of residence
- ☞ Non-residents may need additional documentation

Tram, Milan, Italy

HEALTHCARE IN ITALY
SANITÀ IN ITALIA

Italy's health system is not only free but also excellent. Healthcare in Italy is primarily provided through a universal public healthcare system known as the National Health Service or SSN (*Servizio Sanitario Nazionale*), which gives all Italian citizens and legal residents access to comprehensive and accessible healthcare services, regardless of their financial status. The downside is that waiting times for non-emergency procedures and specialist appointments might be longer for specific procedures due to high demand or limited resources. The SSN partially covers prescription medications. As a patient, you will pay a portion of the cost unless your medications are not covered, in which case you will pay full price.

> Note: In Italy, there is no "Health Insurance" per se, but "Health Coverage" instead.

Primary Care is the foundation of the Italian Healthcare System. It is provided by General Practitioners (GPs) or Family Doctors (*Medici di Base*) who, besides treating patients, refer them to specialists or hospitals when necessary. So, if you need to see a specialist, like a cardiologist or dermatologist, you must check with your GP first. However, go directly to the nearest emergency hospital if you need immediate help. Emergency medical services are provided free of charge to everyone in need. Suppose you need medical assistance at night and can't go to the hospital. In that case, you can call local health services or hospitals to ask about the night doctor (*Medico di Guardia*" or "*Medico Notturn*) in your area. Night doctors are on-call doctors available for emergency medical assistance at the patient's home.

While the Public Healthcare System is the primary provider, there is also a Private Healthcare Sector in Italy. Remember that private healthcare offers faster access to certain services and allows patients to choose their doctors and facilities. So, depending on your needs, you should get private healthcare; not only will you get sooner appointments, but chances to see a doctor who speaks English will be higher. Also, remember that Italy's Healthcare System faces challenges, such as regional disparities in the quality of care, so having alternate insurance can be beneficial.

Finally, Italy participates in the European Health Insurance Card program (EHIC), which allows citizens of European Union (EU) and European Economic Area (EEA) countries to receive necessary healthcare services when visiting Italy.

> Note: The EHIC is often used for temporary stays and tourism.

WHAT YOU NEED TO REGISTER FOR ITALY HEALTH COVERAGE:

To get health coverage in Italy, you will first register with SSN, the Italian National Health Service, at the local Health Departments, ASL (*Azienda Sanitaria Locale*) or USL (*Unità Sanitaria Locale*) to request an Italian Health Card (*Tessera Sanitaria*) and have a doctor assigned.

RESIDENTS

If you are an Italian citizen or a legal resident of Italy, you'll usually need the following documents to register for the National Health Service:

- Tax identification number (*Codice Fiscale*)
- Proof of residency, such as a rental contract or a utility bill in your name
- Valid identification: Passport or ID card
- A health insurance card or one from your home country, if applicable
- Declaration of family composition or a document stating the family members for whom you are registering
- Valid work or residence permit
- A visit to the local Health Authority (ASL) office in your area to complete the registration process

NON-RESIDENTS

(Temporary Stay, Tourists, EU/EEA Citizens, and European Health Insurance Card (EHIC) holders.)

Suppose you are not a resident of Italy but require Healthcare Services during your stay. In that case, the requirements might differ according to your nationality, the duration of your stay, and any bilateral agreements between Italy and your home country.

EU/EEA

EU/EEA citizens can use their European Health Insurance Card (EHIC) for healthcare services. You can get a Provisional Replacement Certificate (PRC) card from your home country if you don't have one.

Non-EU/EEA citizens planning an extended stay might need a Temporary Residency Certificate to access healthcare services by providing a valid identification document, proof of temporary stay including visas, hotel reservations, travel itinerary, or a temporary residence address and a Declaration of Family Composition or a document stating the composition of the family members traveling with you.

ITALY EMERGENCY PHONE NUMBERS:

If, for some reason, you find yourself in a dire situation and need help, Call **112**. This is the **Europe Emergency Number**, accessible anywhere in the EU. Otherwise, you can call:

- Italy State Police (*Carabinieri*): 113
- Italy Medical Emergencies and Ambulance (*Ambulanza*): 118
- Italy Fire Department (*Vigili del fuoco*): 115
- Italy Roadside Assistance (*Assistenza Stradale e Soccorso Stradale*): Automobile Club d'Italia (ACI) 803.116

PHARMACIES IN ITALY

Farmacie

Pharmacies are widely available across cities, towns, and villages in Italy. Pharmacists play a vital role in Italy's healthcare system, providing prescription and over-the-counter medications and information on health and wellness topics, assisting with minor conditions, and recommending appropriate treatments. It's very common in Italy for people to consult a pharmacist before seeing a doctor. You can easily recognize pharmacies by the worldwide green neon cross outside their establishments. Their operating hours vary, but most have regular opening hours during the day. On-duty pharmacies (*Farmacie di Turno*) or night pharmacies (*Farmacie Notturna*) are emergency pharmacies that provide services in case a medical emergency occurs at night or outside regular opening hours. Information about the nearest emergency or nocturnal pharmacy is generally displayed on the pharmacy doors or can be found online. While some pharmacists in larger cities might speak English or other languages, this is not always the case in smaller towns. If you are taking any medication or have prescription pills, try to get at least a three-month refill before you travel to Italy, and bring a doctor's note or a prescription (*Riceta Medica*) with you in case you need a refill before you have your health insurance sorted out.

ALTERNATIVE THERAPIES IN ITALY
Terapie Alternative

Also known as complementary or integrative therapies, alternative therapies are available in Italy alongside conventional medical treatments, with homeopathy being a popular alternative. Many pharmacies in Italy offer homeopathic remedies, and there are trained homeopaths who provide consultations and treatments. You can also consult acupuncturists or doctors who incorporate acupuncture treatments into their practices. Some wellness centers even offer Ayurvedic treatments, including dietary recommendations, massages, and herbal remedies.

Meditation, mindfulness, and yoga are also widely embraced in Italy. However, traditional healing practices or herbal medicine such as Phytotherapy (*Fitoterapia*), and herbal supplements are commonly used in Italy for various health conditions, with different regional herbal remedies passed down through generations.

Note: You should always inform your primary healthcare provider about any alternative therapies you're using to ensure they match or complement your health plan.

MENTAL HEALTHCARE

Assistenza Sanitaria Per La Salute Mentale

Mental healthcare in Italy is provided by a combination of public and private services. There has been increased recognition of the importance of mental health, with various advocacy groups working to reduce stigma and promote mental well-being.

Mental Health Services, including psychiatric care and psychotherapy, are available through the National Health Service (SSN). Primary care doctors play a role in referring individuals to mental health specialists such as psychiatrists, psychologists, psychotherapists, and social workers. Italy has psychiatric hospitals and specialized mental health facilities that offer inpatient and outpatient care for individuals with severe mental health conditions. The focus has shifted from large psychiatric institutions to community-based care and smaller facilities that provide more personalized treatment. For example, Community Mental Health Centers (*Centri di Salute Mentale*) are designed to provide a range of treatments and support for individuals with mental health issues. Many municipalities offer free psychological support services and counseling for individuals dealing with stress, anxiety, or other psychological challenges. The problem for people who do not speak Italian fluently is to find mental health professionals who speak their language. Fortunately, private mental healthcare services are available in Italy, even though it will depend on where you live. The advantage of private healthcare is direct access to psychologists, psychiatrists, and psychotherapists services with no need to see your primary doctor first.

> **Note:** Although there have been improvements, there are still obstacles when it comes to providing equal access to mental healthcare, decreasing stigma, and improving the quality of mental services in Italy. If you or someone you know needs mental healthcare in Italy, contact local healthcare providers or organizations.

MENTAL HEALTHCARE FOR CHILDREN
Assistenza Sanitaria Per La Salute Mentale Dei Bambini

No matter the age of the children, relocating to a new country can be exhilarating and daunting at once. Fear of the unknown, family dynamics, school pressures, and societal changes can all trigger mental health issues, such as anxiety, depression, and behavioral disorders among children and adolescents.

Schools in Italy play a significant role in children's mental health, with some schools implementing mental health programs, workshops, and interventions to promote emotional well-being and resilience in students. Lately, the country has been promoting awareness and anti-bullying campaigns now that it has been proven bullying and cyberbullying can impact children's mental health. If you suspect your child has mental issues, talk to your child's teacher. They are well-trained to recognize signs of mental health issues and support students.

> **Note:** Children's mental health services in Italy are provided through the National Health Service, but access

to specialized care can sometimes be limited due to demand.

Cefalù, Sicily, Italy

LIFE IN ITALY

LA VITA IN ITALIA

Whenever I think of Italy, I am reminded of my Italian brother-in-law's lively and exuberant personality, which always brings a smile to my face. Women in France tend to style their hair in a natural and effortless way as if they just woke up that way. On the other hand, women in Italy often leave their homes with perfectly styled hair that looks as if they just left a hair salon, and Italian men's elegance is undeniable. I will always be in awe of Torino's beautiful architecture and will never stop craving Italian food. However, where you reside in Italy can greatly affect your experience of the country. If you end up living in a region with cold and rainy weather, like Lodi in the Lombardy area, you might find that winter can be unpleasantly rigid despite the country's beauty.

WEATHER

Meteo

Italy has a diverse climate due to its geographic location and varying topography. Coastal areas have milder winters and hotter summers, while inland and mountainous regions may experience more significant temperature variations. Summers can be hot and dry, especially in the southern and central regions and inland areas like Rome and Florence. Every region may get snow in winter, but the frequency and the amount vary greatly depending on altitude and proximity to the sea. The northern areas, including the Italian Alps, experience cold winters with snowfall. If you enjoy winter sports and snow, the Alps provide great skiing and snowboarding opportunities. Out of the 20 regions of Italy, only Apulia does not have at least one alpine ski resort because of the lack of mountains. At the same time, the more southerly you travel, the warmer it tends to be; the Apennines and Central and Southern Italy have milder winters, with coastal areas remaining relatively temperate.

COSTS OF LIVING IN ITALY

Costo Della Vita In Italia

Italy's costs of living are on par with the rest of Europe. According to housinganywhere.com, "Italy is one of the cheapest countries in Western Europe." Suppose you make around 2,000 euros or more; you may need to budget carefully if you rent in major cities such as Milan and Rome, which are among the most expensive Italian towns, and Turin, Palermo, and Naples being the most affordable. For instance, residents of Milan spend more than 40% of their income on rent. On the other hand, their salaries tend to be higher than the rest of the country. However, you can still live comfortably in many parts of the country. For example, for the same price, you can get a spacious one-bedroom apartment (*bilocale*) or a small two-bedroom house in a small town, an average one-bedroom apartment or a studio (*monolocale*) in a big city like Florence, or two tiny bedrooms in a city like Genoa. Once you add the utilities, public transport or gas/fuel, insurance, parking if you own a car, groceries, internet, dining out, entertainment, travel, and maybe private health insurance, how much you spend per month will depend on your status (single or not), location, and lifestyle.

If you are a student or earn the minimum wage in Italy, then life can be challenging, but if you compare it to some parts of the UK or the US, life in Italy is affordable. Students can benefit from affordable housing options available through university housing services or private student residences. If you are single, consider shared accommodation if you're open to living with roommates; sharing an apartment can help you find a more spacious or centrally located place within your budget. Cities in the south, like Naples or Catania, or rural areas, may offer more housing options within your budget because housing remains one of the most significant expenses in Italy.

Ultimately, the key to managing your finances in Italy is creating a detailed budget considering your circumstances and lifestyle choices. It's also a good idea to research the cost of living in your chosen city or region to get a more accurate estimate of your expenses. Doing so will help you adjust your budget accordingly, which will help you cover your basic needs and enjoy your time in the country.

CONSUMER GOODS IN ITALY

Beni Di Consumo In Italia

Italians have the most amazing supermarkets. Even the smallest supermarket has an incredible spread of fruit, vegetables, meat, and cheese; the quality is exceptional because strict food laws prevent excessive preservatives. Moreover, if you want to buy fruits, don't touch them. People will look at you as if you were about to commit a crime because the vendor will either select them for you (you would point to the ones you want) or give you plastic gloves. Italy also has several discount supermarkets, including Lidl and Aldi. The prices for necessities may have increased, but the Italian government has been taking measures to ensure that basic food, such as bread, flour, and milk, remains affordable. On the other hand, prices of cigarettes and beer have increased a lot, while natural resources like fuel, gas, and electricity have remained expensive.

UTILITIES IN ITALY

Servizi Pubblici In Italia

When renting or buying a property in Italy, it's important to remember that utilities' availability, quality, and pricing can vary significantly depending on the region and even within cities. That's why you should always ask about the state of utility services and associated costs. Moreover, it would be best to understand that some utilities may require setting up contracts or registering for services, so contacting the right providers and finding the terms and conditions is advisable.

In most rental agreements, tenants must pay their utility bills separately from their rent. This implies that tenants will have to establish accounts with utility providers and make direct payments for their consumption of electricity, gas, water, and other services. The landlord may help provide instructions on establishing these accounts, but it is the tenant's responsibility to oversee them. On the other hand, an All-Inclusive Rent (*Canone Concordato*) will include all utilities as part of the rent, which means that the tenant pays a fixed monthly rent that covers not only the use of the property but also utilities like water and gas, and electricity, and sometimes even internet and maintenance fees. Usually, these agreements are regulated by local municipalities, which may limit the maximum rent that can be charged but can offer landlords a competitive advantage in the rental market.

> Note: Always check your rights and responsibilities regarding the utilities before buying or renting a property. Determine whether you or the landlord is responsible for setting up and paying for the services.

Electricity (*Elettricità*): In Italy, the electricity system operates on a 230-volt, 50-Hertz system. The primary electricity provider is ENEL (*Ente Nazionale per l'Energia Elettrica*), but you should also consider other regional providers. Once you've selected a supplier, contact them to set up the electricity. You can usually do this through their website, by phone, or by visiting their office in person. In many cases, the provider will arrange for a technician to come and inspect the electricity meter at your property. They will verify that the meter is functioning correctly and may also check its reading. The technician will also activate the electricity supply to your property if it's not connected. You'll need to set up a payment method for your electricity bills. This could be done through direct debit from your bank account or another method specified by your provider. After the electricity is set up, you'll receive monthly or bimonthly bills, depending on your provider and payment plan. The bill will detail your electricity consumption, charges, and payment due date.

Gas (*Gas*): Italy imports a significant portion of its natural gas, mainly from Russia, Algeria, and Norway. Natural gas is widely used for heating and cooking. Since you can choose your gas supplier, you should compare their offers and pricing plans. You can do this online or through official government websites that provide information on energy providers and their rates. As with electricity, once you've selected a gas supplier, contact them to initiate the process. They might schedule a technician to come and inspect the gas meter to ensure it is functioning correctly. The technician may activate the gas supply if it's not connected. After the service is set up, make sure that your bills are paid on time to avoid any service interruptions or late fees. Like electricity, gas bills are usually monthly and are based on consumption. Payment methods can vary, but standard options include bank transfers, direct debit, and online or in-person payments.

Water (*Acqua*): Municipal or regional authorities, known as GIL (*Gestore Idrico Locale*) or a similar name depending on your region, typically manage water supply and sanitation services. Find out which provider serves your area by asking your landlord, checking with neighbors, or searching online, then contact them to request a new water service connection or transfer an existing one. Depending on the circumstances, they may need to inspect your property's water meter and connection. This is more common for new connections or if there are concerns about the existing setup. If an inspection is required, they will schedule a technician to visit your property and verify that the water supply is connected correctly. Water bills are generally issued periodically, and the cost can vary based on usage and location, so check with your local provider for accepted payment options. If you experience any issues with your water supply, such as leaks or problems with water quality, do not hesitate to report them to your local water authority for assistance and resolution.

Even though setting up an electricity, water, and gas bill in Italy is similar, you should contact each provider separately since the required documentation and procedures may vary. Contracts will outline the terms and conditions, billing structure, payment options, and any additional fees associated with each utility.

> **Note**: Try to initiate the setup process well before your move to guarantee that those basic services are in place when you move in, especially if you are moving in during winter.

WHAT YOU NEED TO SET UP GAS, ELECTRICITY AND WATER BILLS IN ITALY:

- Identification and personal documents for all three utilities (electricity, water, and gas)
- Fiscal code
- Proof of address, including a lease agreement, a utility bill in your name from a previous residence, or other documentation confirming your address
- Set up a payment method for your bills. Direct deposit or automatic billing or payments (*addebito diretto*) - or any other method specified by your provider
- Phone number and email address for communication and billing purposes
- Meter readings: if you're renting or buying, your landlord or the previous owner may assist with this step.

In some cases, especially when dealing with local water providers or smaller gas suppliers, you may need to visit the provider's regional office to complete the registration process in person. Always check with the specific utility provider to confirm their requirements.

Santuario Madonna della Corona, Spiazzi, Italy

Waste Collection (*Raccolta Rifiuti*) and recycling are managed locally, so regulations and schedules can vary from one municipality to another. Most cities and towns have specific bins or containers for different types of waste, including organic, recyclable, and non-recyclable materials. Once you know which local municipality or waste management authority is responsible for waste collection in your area, contact them to ask about the waste collection process, the schedule for your area, the requirements, and how to get registered. Waste separation is often mandatory In Italy, so make sure the different types of waste are placed in the appropriate containers. If you miss pickups or the containers get damaged, report these issues to your local waste management authority for resolution. If any fees are associated with waste collection services, you will be responsible for payment. Many stores and supermarkets have small cylindric recipients to collect batteries for free. Cooking oil should not be poured down the sink or into a drain but recycled in a container and dropped at a local collection point. Do not hesitate to ask about proper disposal procedures.

Television And Broadcasting *(Televisione E Radiodiffusione)*: RAI (*Radiotelevisione Italiana*) is the main public service broadcaster and offers a range of television and radio channels. There are also private television networks and cable/satellite TV providers.

Virtual Private Network (*Rete Privata Virtuale*): Using a VPN in Italy doesn't only give you privacy and security, especially if you are a Digital Nomad using public Wi-Fi networks for work; it also gives access to websites, streaming services, and content that may be geographically restricted or inaccessible in Italy. It can also be helpful if you need access to devices and services on your home network while in Italy. If you don't know which VPN to use based on your location, try this website: https://findervpn.com

Internet and Cellphone Services (*Internet e Telecomunicazioni*): Depending on your needs, you can opt for internet and mobile phone plans or prepaid SIM cards in Italy. However, before selecting a service provider, consider the network coverage in the areas you plan to live or visit and compare the provider's data packages and their call and texting rates, especially if you plan to make international calls or send text messages. Depending on your choice of provider, check if you can find them at the airport or retail stores near where you live so that you can set up your phone quickly.

> **Note**: Before traveling, make sure your phone has the frequencies that Italy uses and that your device is unlocked.

The major Internet Service Providers (ISPs) include:

- ☞ TIM (*Telecom Italia Mobile*), a major Italian mobile network provider with extensive nationwide coverage, including rural areas and major cities
- ☞ Vodafone: good network coverage across the country and a reliable service
- ☞ Wind Tre: one of Italy's major mobile network operators, with comprehensive coverage, including urban and rural areas
- ☞ Iliad Italia: competitive pricing, a good choice for budget-conscious travelers

> **Note:** Always check the availability and quality of customer support if you face any issues during your stay.

GETTING AROUND IN ITALY

Muoversi In Italia

As I mentioned earlier, Italians are known for driving fast and close to one another, which unfortunately leads to one of the highest death tolls in Europe. So, while in Italy, you will face erratic drivers, confusing rules, and sometimes crowded roads. Even when walking as a pedestrian, looking both ways before crossing any road is crucial. If you are the driver, be aware of restricted areas or ZTL (*Zona Traffico Limitato*) signs to avoid fines because, while laws may not consistently be enforced, do not expect sympathy from authorities if you commit an infraction.

As I told my friend about writing a book on moving to Italy, he shared an interesting anecdote. He had to spend some time in Italy for work while he lived in the South of France. Since he didn't want to uproot his family, he drove back and forth between the two countries every weekend. As a result, he never changed his license plate. One weekend, he left his car overnight in a parking spot because he couldn't return to France. When he went to get it the following day, there was a market (*a mercato*) where he had parked the car. That's when he noticed a "No parking" (*Vietato Parcheggiare*) sign. Amazingly, his car was still there, surrounded by vendors. When he asked why they didn't tow it away, they explained that it would have been too much of a hassle and helped him drive away safely instead. On the other hand, people have witnessed double-parked cars being thrown over bridges by angry citizens in Italy, causing even more traffic problems.

BUYING A CAR IN ITALY

Comprare Un'auto

As a resident, you can drive in Italy with your driver license or an International Driver's License for up to a year, at which point, you will need to get an Italian driver's license (*Patente*) or have your original license recognized, depending on your country of origin. If you buy a car from a dealership, they will handle all the paperwork. They will mostly ask for your Residence Permit and Tax Number. However, if you plan to purchase a car from a private owner in Italy, you must visit the National Automobile Club (*Automobile Club Italiano*) or ACI, to transfer ownership. It's important to note that all vehicles in Italy are taxed annually, regardless of whether they are new or used and whether you drive them frequently or occasionally. This means that once you own a car, you must pay a yearly Car Tax, also known as "*Bollo.*" So, if you buy a vehicle from a private owner, make sure that the taxes are paid for the rest of the year.

> **Note**: Like many other European countries, Italy operates a points-based system for driving licenses. The points can be deducted for traffic violations, or license suspension or withdrawal.

Additionally, cars in Italy need to undergo check-ups, known as "*Revisione*" or MOT, every two years. Make sure the vehicle you intend to purchase has undergone the check-up or ask when the next one is due. And remember to check the klaxon or horn; you will use it often.

> Note: It won't matter how long you have been driving in your country; you are considered "a new driver" when you get your Italian driver's license.

In Italy, like in many European countries, manual transmission cars (commonly referred to as "stick shift" cars) are common. However, the number of automatic transmission cars has dramatically increased, especially in urban areas. But, since they are less widespread, they cost more. You must be comfortable with the type of transmission you choose, as driving conditions, especially in cities with narrow streets and hilly terrain, can be challenging for those not used to manual transmissions. You will likely not see Ferraris or Lamborghinis, but mostly Opel, Fiat, and Smart cars. And if you must use your phone while driving, use a hands-free device.

> Note: It is illegal to drink and drive if you are over the blood alcohol limit of 0.05% (0.05 grams per deciliter) or 0.5 grams per liter.

TRANSPORTATION IN ITALY
Trasporti

Unless you live in a small village in regions like Sicily or Tuscany, you may not need a car because the country has an excellent public transportation system – buses, trains, trams, ferries, and waterbuses. You can ride a bike; large cities have bike paths, rent electric scooters, share a car ride or walk. Even though public transportation works better in the North, and despite not always being punctual, especially the metro and inter-city transport that can be late or interrupted at times, Italy's public transportation is overall affordable, reliable, and safe, with a train system that offers easy travel throughout the country.

When driving on Italian highways or freeways (*Autostrade*), you will come across toll booths or electronic toll collection systems at the entrance and exit of highways. When entering freeways, you will grab a ticket from the ticket dispensers that you will pay for when you exit. Though most accept major credit cards, some may only take cash. Suppose you can't pay because you don't have any cash; you will call the help button and explain your situation. If they let you go without paying, rest assured that you will get the ticket by mail in the following days. The toll fees contribute to the maintenance and development of the highway infrastructure, and the amount usually varies based on the distance traveled, the type of vehicle, and the specific toll station, which can be public or private. If you plan to use toll roads frequently and don't want to stop at toll booths, you may consider looking into electronic toll payment options or passes, such as *"Telepass,"* and set up automatic payments.

Here are a few useful expressions to get you around:

- *"Camminare"*: To walk
- *"Biglietto del treno/ dell'autobus"*: A train/bus ticket
- *"Una bicicletta"*: A bike
- *"Andare in bicicletta"*: To ride a bike
- *"Una biciletta elettrica"*: An E-bike
- *"Biciclette elettriche"*: Electric bikes
- *"Guidare un'auto"*: To drive a car
- *"Patente di guida"*: Driver's license
- *"Comprare un'auto"*: To buy a car
- *"Noleggiare un'auto"*: To rent a car
- *"Un'auto nuova"*: A new car
- *"Un'auto usata"*: A used car
- *"Volare"*: To Fly
- *"Un aeroplano"*: An airplane
- *"Prendere l'autobus/il treno"*: Take the bus/train

- ☞ *"Sto cercando l'autobus/il treno"*: I am looking for the train/bus station.

- ☞ *"Vorrei comprare un'auto"*: I would like to buy a car. (Vorrei=I would like to)

- ☞ *"Autostrada"*: Highway, freeway

Night View, Amalfi Coast, Italy

REAL ESTATE IN ITALY
Immobiliare In Italia

While driving in the countryside, you might come across rundown properties needing major restoration in what looks like abandoned villages. To attract new residents and restimulate the economy of deserted municipalities, Italy has launched "The One Euro House Program," which allows people over 18 to buy a house for one Euro if the buyer has the funds to restore the house and pay property taxes. If you want to learn more about the program, go to: https://1eurohouses.com/1-euro-houses-map/

Despite the many abandoned properties, finding housing in Italy may be more challenging than one might think because the availability and types of accommodations vary greatly depending on the region and city. If you're looking for housing in urban areas, the most common type available is apartments, ranging from small studios to larger multi-bedroom units. However, if you are searching for a house, you will have to look in suburban or rural areas. And since Italy is known for its historical architecture, with a bit of luck, you may come across unique opportunities in historic buildings or renovated properties. It is important to note that the cost of housing in Italy varies significantly, with cities like Rome, Milan, and Florence having higher rental prices than rural areas. The rental market in these areas can be highly competitive, so it's advisable to start your housing search well in advance. Remember that even within expensive cities or regions, it's possible to find more affordable neighborhoods or nearby towns with a lower cost of living.

Besides the location, rental costs will also depend on the size and condition of the property. That's why, when searching for rental properties, many rely on real estate agencies (*Agenzia Immobiliare*), which typically charge a fee equal to one month's rent or a percentage of the annual rent. Besides real estate agencies, consider reading local newspapers' accommodations sections (*Cerco/Offro Casa Appartamento Stanza*). If you have a car, do not hesitate to drive around looking for "for rent" *(in affitto)* or "for sale" (*in vendita*) signs because many people would rather post or hang signs on their windows than advertise or pay agency fees. Or try Facebook groups where you can look at the ads and maybe find your future home.

It's worth noting that rental agreements (*Contratti di Locazione*) in Italy can vary in length, from short-term (monthly) to long-term (usually three years, renewable), and rental properties can come furnished, partially furnished, or unfurnished. In addition to the rent, tenants are responsible for paying utility bills and sometimes condominium fees (for shared expenses in apartment buildings). So, understand all terms and conditions before signing a lease or rental agreement.

> **Note**: Since some rentals in Italy require a three-year contract, it's best to stay in an Airbnb first and take that time to check out the location.

BUYING PROPERTY IN ITALY

Acquistare Una Proprietà / Comprare Un Immobile

Generally speaking, the Italian real estate market is mainly internal, with Italian property owners selling to Italian buyers. The fact that 85% of Italians are homeowners means that more than half of the population in Italy owns a house. Most Italians don't invest in real estate; they buy houses to live in, no matter their age. This is even more true when you consider that young Italians tend to live with their parents until age 35, and by the time they leave their parent's home, they already have a house waiting to welcome them. That said, the fact more and more foreigners are buying property in Italy means that there is a market for them.

If you plan to buy property in Italy, do your research first and be aware of local housing regulations; research the municipality taxation system and laws that may apply, as some local regulations restrict short-term rentals; remember that taxes and mistakes are common, and the legal system may not always protect buyers. Before making an offer, consider the property's condition, including damage, wear and tear, necessary repairs, and cost. Also, know what can be modified if you plan to remodel or renovate an old house. Just be prepared for the process, which can be highly complex, even for Italians. This complexity of buying a house and the fact that investing in property doesn't qualify for a visa are why foreigners are less likely to buy in Italy. If you don't speak Italian, think of hiring a lawyer who can guarantee the property's legal validity and that all necessary documentation is in order or a translator who can help you with the negotiations.

Despite all of that, buying a property in Italy can be a great investment, even though the location, meaning where you buy, should be the most important factor to consider, as it can affect the value of your investment. When considering areas for investment, it's worth taking into account big cities, tourist areas, and locations with a high number of expats. Properties in those areas will likely be more expensive to buy than those in more rural areas but will end up being more lucrative if you decide to sell, rent, flip, or turn them into an Airbnb.

LANDLORDS

Locatori/Terreni

As a landlord in Italy, you must fulfill some rights, responsibilities, and legal obligations. Typically, rental agreements in Italy are formalized through written contracts. Italian tax laws apply to rental income, meaning you are responsible for reporting and paying taxes. As a landlord, you are responsible for maintaining the property's good condition. This includes making all the necessary repairs, so document the property's condition before and after the rental period, especially if you end up using the tenants' security deposit (*Cauzione*). Italian law regulates rent increases, and you must have legal grounds to evict a tenant. And keep in mind that depending on the location and value of the property, you might have to pay property taxes. If you don't live in Italy or prefer not to handle the property management tasks, you can always hire a property management company to oversee the rental property.

TENANTS/RENTERS

Inquilini/Locatari

The beauty of working remotely or retiring in Italy is that the country possesses a diverse range of cities and regions, each with its unique housing market and pricing. It's important to remember that rental prices can fluctuate over time, and the availability of rental properties can vary depending on the demand in your chosen area. Additionally, a rental property's specific features, size, and condition can affect its monthly rent. Older or less modern apartments may be more affordable than newly renovated ones. Similarly, properties with fewer amenities may have lower rents. If you decide to rent in a major city suburb, you may have a higher chance of finding something within your budget; only be prepared for a longer commute to the city center.

If you are flexible with your preferences, consider smaller towns or rural areas that fit your budget better. Medium-sized cities such as Bologna, Genoa, or Palermo, as well as certain regions in southern Italy like Naples or Catania, offer a wider range of rental options due to the lower living costs. Consider using online real estate websites or working with a local real estate agent, especially if your Italian is limited, to find the best rental property that meets your needs. They can also assist with negotiations and understanding the terms and conditions of the rental agreement, such as local taxes or fees associated with rentals. Lastly, familiarize yourself with your rights and protections as a tenant and consider rental insurance to protect your belongings. Landlords often require a security deposit that should be returned at the end of the lease, provided there is no damage or unpaid rent. In many cases, utility costs (water, gas, electricity) are separate from the rent and are the tenant's responsibility.

> **Note:** In Italy, a gated residence is often referred to as a "fenced residence" (*Residenza Recintata*) or "an enclosed residential complex (*Complesso Residenziale Recintato*).

To help you communicate your housing needs more accurately with landlords, real estate agents, or property search platforms, here are a few expressions:

- "*Locatori/ Terreni*": Landlords
- "*Inquilini/Locatari*": Tenants
- "*Casa*": House
- "*Appartamento*": Appartment
- "*Duplex*": Duplex
- "*Villa*": Villa
- "*Residenza recintata*": Gated residence
- "*Casa nuova*": New house
- "*Casa vecchia*": Old house
- "*Contratto di locazione*": A lease or rental agreement
- "*Contratto*": A contract or an agreement
- "*Coinquilini*": Roommates
- "*Sto cercando un monolocale*": I am looking for a studio apartment.
- "*Sto cercando un bilocale*": I am looking for a one-bedroom apartment.
- "*Arredato*": Furnished
- "*Non arredato*": Unfurnished
- "*Cauzione*": Security Deposit

☞ *"Agenzia Immobiliare": Real Estate Agency*

☞ *"Imposta Municipale Unica": Property Taxes*

Genoa, Italy

CITIZENSHIP IN ITALY
CITTADINANZA IN ITALIA

In Italy, becoming a citizen is based on residency, ancestry, marriage, or other long-term circumstances. Italy also offers a pathway to citizenship to legal residents who have lived there for a specific number of years, often ten years, while holding a valid Residence Permit. Requirements can vary based on family ties, language proficiency, and employment history. The process is typically overseen by the local *"Prefettura"* or other relevant immigration offices.

WHAT YOU NEED TO APPLY FOR CITIZENSHIP IN ITALY:

- ☞ Completed application forms
- ☞ A copy of your valid passport and any previous passports, if applicable
- ☞ Copies of your valid residence permit showing your legal residence in Italy
- ☞ A certified copy of your marriage certificate to prove the legality of your union, if your application is based on marriage
- ☞ Birth certificate, translated into Italian if it's in a different language, if applicable

- ☞ A sworn statement declaring that you have not been convicted of certain crimes in your home country or countries of previous residence or that you have no criminal record or any pending charges, if applicable
- ☞ Proof of basic Italian language proficiency (language course certificates or test results), if applicable
- ☞ Recent passport-sized photographs
- ☞ A statement explaining your integration into Italian society, your ties to the community, and your knowledge of Italian culture
- ☞ Documents that demonstrate that you have the means to support yourself and your family in Italy (pay stubs, bank statements, job contracts...)
- ☞ A certificate stating that you are in good health and have no contagious diseases
- ☞ The required fee for processing your citizenship application
- ☞ Proof of lineage if your demand is based on ancestry

Once you have submitted all the documents, the Italian authorities will conduct background checks to ensure you have no criminal record. They will also review your application and supporting documents, and if approved, you will be granted Italian citizenship.

> **Note:** If your application is successful, you may be invited to attend a naturalization ceremony to receive your citizenship certificate.

ITALIAN CITIZENSHIP THROUGH MARRIAGE

Cittadinanza Per Matrimonio

You must meet some requirements before applying for Italian citizenship through marriage. For instance, you must have lived legally in Italy for at least two years. This period may be extended to three years if you live abroad with your Italian spouse. You also must hold a valid Residence Permit during your time in Italy. Some regions in Italy may require you to demonstrate a basic proficiency in the Italian language, which can be done through a language test or course. Usually, one doesn't need to be fluent in Italian to get citizenship through marriage. However, your marriage must have been legally recognized and ongoing throughout the residency period, which means it will be harder to gain citizenship if you get divorced before getting your citizenship.

If you meet all these requirements, you will apply to the appropriate authorities with the supporting documents. Remember that the application forms and required documents (see list above) can vary based on your specific situation and the region you are applying to. Sometimes, you may be required to attend an interview to discuss your marriage and integration into Italian society.

ITALIAN CITIZENSHIP THROUGH RESIDENCY OR NATURALIZATION

Cittadinanza Per Residenza

Acquiring citizenship through residency involves becoming a citizen of Italy after fulfilling specific residency requirements and meeting certain criteria, such as having legally resided in the country for ten years. However, those requirements might be reduced to five years of residency if you are a refugee or stateless person and four years if you are an EU long-term resident. You must also prove that you can support yourself and your family without relying on public funds. Some regions in Italy may require you to demonstrate a basic level of proficiency in the Italian language, which can be proven through a language test or course completion certificate. You should demonstrate integration into Italian society, familiarity with Italian culture and customs, and have a clean criminal record and good moral character. You will complete and submit the Italian Citizenship through Residency application forms and provide the required supporting documents (see list above). Depending on the region and circumstances, you might be required to attend an interview to discuss your integration and eligibility.

> Note: Gaining citizenship takes at least a decade of legally working and living in Italy. The Italian government can reject an application if they suspect the person is a risk to the country.

CITIZENSHIP BASED ON ANCESTRY OR BY DESCENT

Cittadinanza Basata Su Un'ascendenza

Getting citizenship through ancestry (*Jus Sanguinis*) involves becoming a citizen of a country based on your family connections to citizens of that country, meaning you may be eligible for Italian citizenship if you have Italian ancestors, which typically includes parents, grandparents, and sometimes great-grandparents. However, your lineage should be uninterrupted, meaning if your Italian ancestor became a citizen of another country before the birth of your parents, you might not qualify. I have known a few Argentinians who have gained Italian citizenship this way. So, if you are eligible, you should gather the necessary documents tracing back to your Italian ancestors to prove your relationship: birth certificates, marriage certificates, and other vital records that establish your lineage.

> Note: If you have none of these documents but know which part of Italy your ancestor was from, remember that town halls, municipalities, administration offices, parishes, and churches all have stored data and recordings from family names, marriages, births, and deaths dating from centuries ago.

Once you have gathered all the documentation, you should submit your application for Italian Citizenship through Ancestry. This usually involves completing the appropriate forms and providing the required supporting documents. Some regions might require you to prove your intention to live in Italy. This can often be done by registering your residence with the local authorities.

> Note: The requirements and processes can vary based on specific circumstances, such as the generation of Italian ancestors, your place of residence, and changes in Italian citizenship laws.

DUAL CITIZENSHIP

Doppia Cittadinanza / Cittadinanza Doppia

Italian law does not require you to give up your citizenship from your country of origin. However, dual citizenship may not be an option if your country only allows one citizenship. Some people would rather have Italian citizenship for the benefits of an EU passport. In contrast, others might struggle with the idea. I knew a man who refused French citizenship because he was still attached to his country of origin. However, when one of his children moved to Canada, he realized he needed a visa to visit because his country of origin didn't have visa-free agreements with Canada.

> Note: Dual Citizenship allows you to get an Italian passport, and you won't have to pay taxes on any income you earn outside the country.

Sorrento, Italy

WHERE TO LIVE IN ITALY

DOVE VIVERE IN ITALIA

There are 20 administrative regions in Italy, Abruzzo, Basilicata, Calabria, Campania, Emilia-Romagna, Friuli-Venezia Giulia, Lazio, Liguria, Lombardy, Marche, Molise, Piedmont, Apulia (Puglia), Sardinia (Sardegna), Sicily (Sicilia), Tuscany (Toscana), Trentino-Alto Adige (Trentino-South Tyrol), Umbria, Aosta Valley (Valle d'Aosta) and Veneto. Moreover, each region is further divided into provinces. Besides personal preferences – beachside or countryside – when choosing a place to live in Italy, consider factors such as internet connectivity if you work from home, costs of living, the weather, proximity to hospitals or specialized doctors, school choices, and a reliable transportation system. Remember that a place with many expats means fewer chances to feel isolated. They will not only provide a support system but will help with integration, too. However, the downside is finding yourself hanging out exclusively with other foreigners and not getting to know locals.

If you or a family member has mobility issues, you might want to stay away from hilly areas or places with uneven ground, cobblestone streets, and limited accessible transportation options. Also, visiting potential locations and talking to locals before committing to a place can be a good idea. Italy is beautiful, the weather is great, but winters can be cold, especially if you decide to buy an old house, because chances are it might not have a heating system. Like any other country, big cities such as Rome, Milan, or Florence will be more welcoming and diverse than small towns.

Piedmont, Italy

NORTHERN ITALY

Italia Settentrionale / Nord Italia

Northern Italy is not only the "economic powerhouse of the country," but it is said to be cleaner and generally more organized. It is home to major cities like Milan, Turin, and Genoa. Northern Italy offers diverse landscapes, including the Italian Alps in the north, the Italian Lakes region (Lake Como, Lake Maggiore, Lake Garda), and the picturesque regions of Tuscany or Emilia-Romagna.

EMILIA-ROMAGNA REGION

Bologna – La Rossa – is the capital city of the Emilia-Romana Region. It is a lovely middle town near the Italian Apennine Mountain. Thanks to the University of Bologna, the city has a vibrant student population that contributes to the lively atmosphere, its historic charm, and the growing number of co-working spaces. Bologna offers a high quality of life and relatively good employment opportunities. It's also a great place for families, because though it is a big city, it is not very large, making it very walkable to the point where you might not need a car to live here because the transport system is good and usually on time.

> **Note**: Bolognese sauce (*Ragù alla Bolognese*) originated from Bologna.

THE LIGURIA REGION – THE ITALIAN RIVIERA

This narrow coastal crescent-shaped region in northwestern Italy borders France to the west, Piedmont to the north, and Tuscany to the east. It is famous for the Cinque Terre villages - Riomaggiore, Manarola, Corniglia, Vernazza, and Monterosso al Mare – a collection of five colorful fishing villages perched on cliffs along the coastline. The villages are UNESCO World Heritage Sites known for their scenic beauty, hiking trails, and delectable local cuisine; many Italian culinary delights, such as pesto, focaccia, and parmesan cheese, originated here.

However, if you are considering relocating to the Cinque Terre, look for Levanto, a charming coastal town in the Liguria region. Although it is not one of the five villages, it is often called the unofficial "sixth" village due to its proximity and accessibility to the area since it is just north of the official Cinque Terre villages. Levanto is known for being more relaxed and less crowded than the other villages and boasts a beautiful sandy beach, in contrast to some of the rocky beaches found in the Cinque Terre. The town has a charming historic center with picturesque narrow streets, colorful buildings, and a lively atmosphere. It is well-connected by train, making it easy to travel to the neighboring villages and other towns in Liguria and Tuscany. Portofino, a charming coastal town, is another well-known destination in Liguria with a picturesque harbor, upscale boutiques, and beautiful hiking trails in Portofino Regional Natural Park.

Genoa, Genova, Genes – La Superba – is the birthplace of Christopher Columbus, the capital of the Liguria Region, and one of Italy's latest hidden gems. Life is quiet in Genes, the cost of living is low, and the many outdoor activities make it a perfect place for families. It is a medium-sized city with great weather, not overly provincial or expensive, and without the complications of large cities. Many remote workers are buying property in Genoa because it is one hour and a half away from Turin and Milan and has an international airport. Also, living in Genova means living by the sea since it has a bustling seaport. It is also two hours from the Alps, the French Côte d'Azur, Tuscany, Corsica, and Sardinia. However, if you decide to settle there, make sure your Italian is solid because, though quite multicultural, most of the inhabitants are senior citizens who don't speak English.

> **Note:** Jeans originated from Genes, and so did pesto.

LOMBARDIA – LOMBARDY REGION

Milan, Milano – Italy's Business Center – is the capital city of the Lombardi Region and of the province of Milan. It is a big, touristy city with a thriving economy and a strong focus on technology. The city also offers a range of co-working spaces, a large community of expats, and a fast-paced urban environment with various options for public transportation. However, you can't write about Milan without mentioning Italy's two main soccer/football leagues: AC Milan (*Associazione Calcio Milan*) and Inter Milan (*Internazionale Milan*). To tell the difference between the two teams: AC Milan was founded by two Englishmen who forbade non-Italian players from joining. Inter Milan was created a couple of years later by former AC Milan members and adopted an "all non-Italian players are welcome" policy.

> **Note:** AC Milan fans were commonly known as screwdrivers (*Casciavit*), which is derived from a Milanese dialect. The name also referenced their working-class origins, as many were blue-collar workers. On the other hand, Inter Milan fans were often referred to as "boasters" (*Bauscia*). This was because they were seen as more affluent and typically came from the wealthy northern suburbs of Milan.

Lake Como – Lago di Como – is one of the most famous and picturesque lakes in the Lombardy region and was home to the actor George Clooney for many years before he decided to sell his property. This picturesque region is a quieter option for remote work with its stunning landscape, charming lakeside towns, luxurious villas, and natural beauty.

THE VENETO REGION – LA SERENISSIMA

Padua – Padova – is just a short train ride from Venice in the Veneto Region. It is one of the oldest cities in Italy and is home to one of the most prestigious and renowned universities in the country, The University of Padua, which was founded in 1222. The Basilica of Saint Anthony of Padua (*Basilica di Sant'Antonio*) is a significant pilgrimage site. Padua is also home to the world's oldest academic botanical garden (*Orto Botanico di Padova*), which was established in 1545. It is a UNESCO World Heritage Site and houses a vast collection of plants from around the world. Padua is easily accessible by train from major Italian cities and can be reached by road.

Venice, Venezia – The Floating City – is home to the Venice International Movie Festival. Venice is a unique city in the Veneto Region as it is made up of 118 small islands separated by 150 canals. The city, which has been sinking, offers a unique setting for remote work with its canals, art, rich history, romantic atmosphere, and less noise due to the absence of cars. However, although quiet during the offseason, it can get overcrowded and unbearable during tourist peak seasons, coinciding with the hottest and most humid time of the year. If you can't tolerate the crowd or the humidity, be reassured because Venice has an international airport and a great train system that allows a quick escape to other European countries.

Unfortunately, during the fall and winter seasons, increased water levels in the canals often lead to flooding in the city, something to keep in mind if you find yourself living on the ground floor. A noticeable odor will also arise from the sewage in the canals during low water levels. If you choose to live in Venice, you may rely on waterbuses to get you around daily since they remain the city's least expensive means of transport, with residents getting preferential prices. Talking about residents, most of the people you will meet in Venice live on the mainland and are only there for work.

> **Note**: You can't ride a bike, skateboard, or roller-skate in Venice. Instead of cars, Venetians use gondolas, waterbuses, or their feet.

Marche Region, Italy

CENTRAL ITALY
Italia Centrale

ABRUZZO REGION – THE LUNGS OF EUROPE

The region is home to several national parks and is only 2 hours away from Rome. It is a paradise for nature enthusiasts, with mountain biking, rock climbing, and wildlife observation opportunities. It is home to the Apennine Mountains, boasts a long coastline along the Adriatic Sea, and is accessible by train and road, with major highways connecting it to other parts of Italy. The region's main airport, Abruzzo Airport, is in Pescara, the largest town in the region, and offers connections to several European cities. However, if I were to decide where to live in the region, I would probably choose the city of Chieti, pronounced "Kee-yay-tee," the capital of the province of Chieti in the Abruzzo region. Though less populated, it remains more attractive with its mix of historical and modern attractions. Considered one of the oldest towns in Italy, it is said to have been settled by Achilles and was named after his mother, Theate. It is a lively town with festivals and concerts. The theater, *"Teatro Marrucino,"* hosts performances ranging from classical music to contemporary plays, and the University of Chieti-Pescara, officially known as "G. D'Annunzio University," is one of Italy's prominent universities.

THE LAZIO REGION – LATIUM

Located in the central portion of the peninsula, Lazio comprises five provinces, one of them being Italy's largest city and capital, Roma – the Eternal City (*Città Eterna*) – which also happens to be the capital of the Lazio region. Besides Rome, Lazio is mostly rural, with charming stone-built villages, historic landmarks, hiking trails. Like any large European city, Rome has something for everyone: a vibrant atmosphere, historical sites, international schools and airports, good hospitals, a mix of traditional and modern amenities, and Tivoli is only over half-an hour away by car. The city also offers many co-working spaces and cafes with Wi-Fi, making it the ideal place for remote work. The only downside is that everything costs more in Rome, not to mention air pollution and littering in some tourist areas, unless you choose to live in one of the other Lazio provinces: Frosinone, Latina, Rieti or Viterbo.

MARCHE REGION – LE MARCHE – THE OTHER TUSCANY

Marche Region is in the central part of the country along the eastern side, facing the Adriatic Sea. It is tucked between the Abruzzo and Emilia-Romagna and borders Tuscany and Umbria on the west. It is the sixth smallest region in Italy and the eighth smallest in population. Ancona is the capital city, and Urbino, another province, is a UNESCO World Heritage Site known for Renaissance art and culture. Rafaello, the artist, was born here. Though no longer a hidden gem, it has recently been put back on the map after going through a decline in population. Try to stay in the central or coastal area, where you will enjoy warmer temperatures and find most English-speaking communities. Le Marche has everything one needs to enjoy life in Italy and can be a great retirement spot. Hop on a bus, and you are on your way to Florence or Rome, and Ancona has an airport. Besides art and culture, life remains quite affordable in Le Marche. You can play golf, ride a horse, hike, dance, or go to the beach. The downside is that you will probably need a car if you choose to live in the region, also known for its wine production.

> **Note**: Most of Italy's luxury shoes are manufactured in this region, and the inhabitants are called "*Marchigiani*."

TUSCANY – TOSCANA – THE GREEN HEART OF ITALY

If you choose to live in "*Il Cuore Verde D'italia*," consider living in the countryside for a more rural and tranquil atmosphere, unless you rely on internet access for work. That's because Tuscany's countryside offers picturesque landscapes, vineyards, and historic towns. Next to it is the Tuscan Archipelago, a chain of Islands; among them are Elba, the small island where Napoleon was exiled, and Montecristo, a rugged and inaccessible island made famous thanks to "The Count of Montecristo," the novel by French author Alexander Dumas. However, it's the novel "Under the Tuscan Sun" that made it famous among Americans, who now form one of the most significant expat communities in the region.

Florence, Firenze – The Cradle of the Renaissance (*La Culla Del Rinascimento*) – is the capital city and the most visited city in Tuscany. It is rich in culture and history, with a wide selection of co-working spaces, reliable internet connectivity, bilingual schools, with the International School of Florence being the main one, and a large British community; most digital nomads in Florence choose to live in Santo Spirito because of the high number of ex-pats.

> **Note**: Vinci, a small town west of Florence, is none other than the birthplace of Leonardo Da Vinci.

Siena – City of the Palio – is the second largest city in Tuscany after Florence and is about an hour south of the capital city, to the southwest of the Chianti region. Despite the high cost of rent and groceries, Siena remains an attractive option for those considering moving to the area. The locals are fluent in English, so language should not be a barrier until you visit local stores. Apart from its rich history, this medium-sized walled city has a university, cobblestone streets, cafes, a magnificent marketplace, the "*Piazza Del Campo*," which hosts the famous horse races (*Palio De Siena*), excellent restaurants, and one of the most stunning cathedrals in Tuscany. Although Siena does not have an international airport, the transportation system is excellent, and the nearest airport in Florence is easily accessible by train, providing access to the rest of Italy and Europe.

THE CHIANTI REGION – THE HEART OF TUSCANY

If you plan to live in Tuscany, try this wine-producing area between the cities of Florence and Siena, which has given its name to one of Italy's most famous red wines, the Chianti wine. Known for its picturesque landscapes, rolling hills, and charming towns, the region provides an amazing agro-tourism experience while boasting a big community of expats, mostly retirees. The small, picturesque town of Greve, located in the center of the region, is a notable destination for nomads and tourists alike. Unfortunately, being a small town also means limited access to services you find in larger cities, such as hospitals, schools, stores, and cultural events or services. While Greve is well-connected by road to other parts of Tuscany, the transportation options are also limited, especially if you are a frequent traveler and need easy access to an airport. Lamole is another small town in the Chianti hills that offers breathtaking views of the surrounding vineyards, olive groves, and woodlands. Despite being one of the smallest towns in Italy, it is a peaceful and popular destination, perfect for writers and artists looking for inspiration or anyone looking for a quiet life.

Tuscany, Italy

SOUTHERN ITALY

Mezzogiorno / Italia Meridionale

"*Mezzogiorno*" means "midday" because the sun is at its zenith or highest around noon in the southern part of the country. Southern Italy includes Campania, Calabria, Apulia, Basilicata, and Sicily. The term "*Mezzogiorno*" is not just a geographical designation but also carries cultural, historical, and economic implications, representing a distinctive part of Italy with its own traditions, dialects, and historical development. Southern Italy has a rich history influenced by various civilizations such as the Greeks, Romans, Byzantines, Normans, and Arabs. This cultural blend has had a lasting impact on the region's architecture, traditions, and cuisine. The weather is mostly Mediterranean, which means that summers are hot and dry, and winters are mild and wet. The region is renowned for its focus on fresh and locally sourced ingredients.

Located at the "toe" of Italy's boot, Campania is famous for its pizza and pasta dishes like "*spaghetti alla puttanesca.*" The region is very touristy, with a beautiful coastline and rugged mountains. Sicily, the largest island in the Mediterranean, is renowned for the cities of Palermo and Catania and its archaeological sites, such as the Valley of the Temples. Although Sardinia is not part of the Italian mainland, it's often classified as Southern Italy due to its location. Living in Sicily (or Sardinia) can make some people feel confined, which is more accurate for those suffering from claustrophobia. So, before making a move, make sure you are comfortable with the idea that it will take a boat ride or a flight to get off the islands.

CAMPANIA REGION – TERRA FELIX – FERTILE LAND – HAPPY LAND

The Amalfi Coast – Costiera Amalfitana – is a stunning coastal area that stretches along the southern coast of the Sorrentine Peninsula in the Province of Salerno in Campania. The coast consists of the towns of Amalfi, the city that gave the coast its name, Positano, a popular and glamorous destination, Ravello, perched high in the hills, the serene Praiano and Sorrento, technically not part of the Amalfi Coast but serves as a gateway to the region and remains a lovely coastal town. Each town has unique characteristics and is known for its architecture, beaches, cultural attractions, breathtaking views, and peaceful environment. Apart from swimming and water sports, the Coast provides a range of outdoor activities, including hiking along the famous scenic trail called "The Path of the Gods" or "*Sentiero degli Dei.*" It is accessible by the Amalfi Drive (*Strada Statale 163*), a famous and scenic coastal road, and has public buses and ferries that connect the coastal towns. Keep in mind that it is a popular destination for international travelers, which can result in congested roads, busy towns, limited parking, crowded buses and ferries, and varying internet connectivity, depending on your location.

Naples, Napoli – The Soul of Italy – is the capital city of the Campania Region and one of Italy's oldest cities. It was founded by the Greeks, who named it "New City" (*Neápolis*). It is the birthplace of pizza and renowned composers like Puccini and Verdi and is just a short distance from Mount Vesuvius and Pompei. The city is a maze of narrow streets and alleys that cause traffic issues and noise problems. You will find colorful but decaying buildings, historical sites, fantastic art, shops, street markets, a vibrant culture, and natural beauty. The Bay offers breathtaking views of Capri, Ischia, Procida, Vesuvius, and the Amalfi Coast. Downtown Naples, a UNESCO World Heritage Site, is one of Europe's most densely populated and vibrant city centers. The city has inspired the saying *"Vedi Napoli e poi muori,"* meaning "See Naples and die." This is because it is a stunning and captivating place to see. However, nowadays, it can be described as a combination of grandeur and urban chaos, even though some will say that the chaos is part of its charm. Like most southern Italian cities, the cost of living in Naples is much lower than in Rome, Milan, and Florence, and so is the average monthly salary. It is also cheaper to rent or buy property in Naples than in Rome. The International School of Naples is centrally located and offers tuition in English and Italian. The High-Speed Train (*Treno Alta Velocità*) will take you to Rome in one hour from the main train station (*Napoli Centrale*). If you love history or food or want an authentic Italian experience, Naples is probably the place to be.

CALABRIA REGION

Calabria is at the southernmost tip of the booted country, where the toes should be, between the Amalfi Coast and Sicily. The region includes several cities and towns, with Reggio Calabria and Cosenza being the most significant cities. For a long time, Calabria was overlooked by foreigners, which has prompted the local government to launch a three-year program, "the Active Residency Project," to revitalize the small villages that have been abandoned. The program aimed to attract individuals under 40 who are willing to start a small business and relocate to one of the twelve villages in the Calabria region, which has a population of less than 2,000. A group of creative professionals, "*La Rivoluzione delle Seppie,*" even set up co-working spaces in the village of Belmondo Calabro to encourage remote workers to move to the area.

PUGLIA REGION – APULIA

Puglia is located at the "heel" of Italy's boot, in the southern part of Italy. It is known for its charming towns, unique architecture with whitewashed conical roofed "*Trulli*" houses in Alberobello, and stunning coastline along the Adriatic Sea. It has a relaxed atmosphere and has seen a growing interest among digital nomads. Two of its towns, Presisce and Acquarica, will pay new residents to move there and buy or renovate a house. Puglia is famous for its Mediterranean cuisine, featuring abundant fresh seafood, olive oil, wine, and pasta. Dishes like "*orecchiette*" and local specialties such as burrata cheese and extra virgin olive oil (*olio extra vergine di oliva*) are popular.

SARDINIA – SARDEGNA – ISOLA DEL SOLE – ISLAND OF THE SUN

Sardinia is a large Italian island in the Mediterranean Sea known for its beautiful beaches and natural landscapes, and it is a popular summer vacation for Italians. Unfortunately, like the rest of the country, it has seen its youth leave because of the lack of employment opportunities. To fight the effect of depopulation, the island has offered to pay anyone willing to move there permanently to buy or renovate a house, preferably in a municipality with less than 3,000 residents.

Cagliari, a coastal town and the capital of Sardinia, offers a peaceful environment for remote work. It has slightly humid winters but long and lovely summers that can last until mid-October. If you choose to live in Cagliari, you will experience a laid-back and stress-free life. Not only are the costs of living lower than in most Italian cities, but the quality of their products is exceptional, too. However, remember that a low cost of living also means low wages. Another downside of living in Cagliari is the travel. You will have to depend on ferries and flights to leave the island, which means planning for each trip. It takes 8 to 16 hours to reach Rome, Naples, Genoa, or Palermo by boat. Thankfully, the largest airport, Cagliari Elmas Airport (CAG), has direct flights to mainland Italy and other European cities.

> **Note**: Cagliari is built on hills, so be ready to walk uphill most of the time, which is not ideal if you have difficulties walking.

SICILY – TRINACRIA – THE ISLAND WITH THREE HEADLANDS

Sicily is the largest island in the Mediterranean, way larger than Malta, both in terms of land area: 25,711 square kilometers (9,927 square miles) vs 316 square kilometers (122 square miles), and population. The largest region of Italy, it is at a crossroads between continents (Europe, North Africa, and the Middle East) and part of the Ionian region and the Ionian Sea. The island has its own culture, traditions, and dialect (Sicilian), which differs from the Italian language. It is home to Mount Etna and has nine provinces to choose from. The nickname "*Trinacria*" comes from an ancient Greek name, a reference to Sicily's triangular shape, which is formed by three capes: Capo Peloro in the northeast, Capo Passero in the southeast, and Capo Lilibeo in the west. There are few job opportunities in Sicily, and if you plan to open a company, be aware that taxes are pretty high, even for small and medium-sized enterprises (SMEs) and startups.

Palermo is the capital city of Sicily. If you prefer a lifestyle that includes the coast and the Mediterranean, this city has a lot to offer. If the cost of living is affordable, rental prices can be expensive. The infrastructure is not great, and people are often forced to use their cars, which can result in traffic and parking issues. Like the rest of the country, bureaucracy remains a significant problem, with few online services available. There are some excellent hospitals, but as with any city, it's always best to ask around before choosing a specific doctor. However, with its stunning landscapes, a relaxed pace of life, and a growing number of digital nomads and expat communities, Palermo is worth considering. It is the warmest major city in Italy, with mild winters and hot summers, and the locals are known for being quite friendly. There is a large university, which provides a vibrant nightlife, and as expected from Italy, the food is excellent.

Whether drawn to the bustling urban centers, the tranquil countryside, or the sun-kissed coastal regions, Italy offers a wide variety of regions, cities, and villages to choose from, depending on your needs, wants, and means. However, to truly explore and appreciate the country, one must also learn to appreciate the subtle nuances in lifestyle and customs, such as the warmth of Southern hospitality differing from the dynamic spirit in the North. Each region has its unique identity shaped by Italy's rich history, delectable cuisine, and warm-hearted people who create an inviting atmosphere for anyone looking to add a new and exciting phase to their lives.

ONE LAST WORD

Whether it becomes your forever home or a stepping-stone to new adventures, moving to Italy is more than getting a new address; it's about embracing a lifestyle that goes beyond the beautiful scenery and historic landmarks and finding comfort in simple pleasures. Italy's focus on work-life balance, family values, and a slower-paced lifestyle offers a refreshing change for anyone looking for a more relaxed and fulfilling life. And if Italy isn't your final stop, there are countless other destinations to explore - from Portugal and Spain to the tropical paradise of Bali. Home is where the heart is, and Italy will welcome you with open arms if you are willing to make it your home.

Once again, whether you have done it already or not, I would be honored if you could take a moment and leave a review to help guide others and enrich our collective experience. Visit the following page by scanning the QR code or the platform you got the book from and share your thoughts. And before you close the book, test your knowledge, and see how much you know about Italy. Thank you for being a part of my journey and helping me make your adventure meaningful.

"The future belongs to those who believe in the beauty of their dreams."

- Eleanor Roosevelt

TEST YOUR KNOWLEDGE
TESTA LA TUA CONOSCENZA

1. Italy is part of the EU, the Schengen area, and the Single Market. Y/N
2. Which Italian region is categorized as a Blue Zone?
3. How do you say Dad in Italian? *Papa* or *Papà*?
4. What system allows citizens of certain countries to apply for a Schengen Visa online for short-term stays of up to 90 days?
5. An ESTIAS is a mandatory visa waiver for anyone traveling to Europe. Y/N
6. Whether you need a visa or not to enter Italy will depend on your nationality, Italian immigration policies, and the purpose and duration of your trip. Y/N
7. Who gets to decide whether you can be permitted to enter Italy?
8. Who can apply for a Schengen Visa?
9. How old should a child be to be exempted from paying Schengen Visa fees?
10. Are Italy's Long-Stay Visas and National Visas the same? Y/N
11. Name other types of lodging in Italy besides Airbnb and hotels.

12. Which visas are available for a digital nomad wishing to live in Italy?

13. What document allows you to work in Italy?

14. Anyone can apply for an EU Blue Card. Y/N

15. How many types of high schools are there in Italy?

16. Can you work in Italy with an Elective visa? Y/N

17. What is the Italy Remote Work Visa?

18. What is SPID?

19. What is a "*Questura*"?

20. What are other names for a "*Nulla Osta*"?

21. What was Italy's currency before the euro?

22. What is Italy's Tax Identification Number comprised of?

23. What does SSN stand for?

24. Can you apply for an Investor Visa when you buy property in Italy?

25. Italy has 20 administrative regions. Can you name at least 5?

26. Why one should think twice before living in Sardinia or Sicily?

27. What Italian region is called the "*Mezzogiorno?*"

28. Buying property in Italy is a bad idea.

ANSWERS

RISPOSTE

1. YES. Part of the European Union (EU) (a political and economic union of member states located primarily in Europe,) Italy is also a member of the Schengen Area (a zone comprising European countries that have abolished passport control at their mutual borders), and the Single Market (the free movement of goods, services, capital, and people within the EU).
2. Italy has been recognized for having relatively high life expectancies, with Sardinia being one of the "Blue Zones" in the world.
3. *"Papa"* (Pope) / *"Papà"* (Dad)
4. The Electronic Visa Application System (EVAS) allows citizens of certain countries to apply for a Schengen Visa online for short-term stays of up to 90 days.
5. NO. Only visa-free travelers from outside the Schengen Area who wish to travel to Italy for a maximum stay of 90 days within 180 days must complete a simple online application to receive a mandatory visa waiver or an ESTIAS (European Travel Information and Authorization System).

6. YES. Whether you need a visa or not to enter Italy will depend on your nationality, Italian immigration policies, and the purpose and duration of your trip.

7. Even with an approved visa, it's the Border Officer who makes the final decision on whether you shall be permitted to enter Italy or not.

8. The Schengen Visa or Type C Visa is for non-EU citizens traveling for a short period to a European Union country and whose country does not have a visa-free agreement with the Schengen States.

9. Children under the age of six are exempted from Schengen visa fees.

10. The Italy National Visa, another term for the Italy Long-Stay Visa, is a generic visa for staying in Italy for over 90 days.

11. "Scattered or dispersed hotels," commonly known as *"Albergi Diffusi,"* provide a unique and charming way to experience Italian culture, history, and rural life. A Pension Hotel (*Pensione*) or an inn (*Pensionato Albergo*) are often family-run establishments that provide accommodations and sometimes meals to travelers, while Co-living spaces are a modern form of housing where like-minded people share a living space.

12. A Digital Nomad can apply for an Investor, Self-employment, Start-up Visa, or Nomad Visa to live and work in Italy.

13. Non-EU/EEA citizens need a Work Permit to work in Italy.

14. NO. The EU Blue Card doubles as a Work Visa and Residency Permit for Highly Qualified Workers from non-EU countries.

15. Students in Italy can choose from 3 types of high schools based on their goals.

16. NO. The Italian Elective Residence visa does not allow you to work or seek employment under any conditions. You will need to switch to a Work visa if you decide to come out of retirement.

17. The Italy Digital Nomad Visa is also called the Remote Work Visa.

18. The Public System for Digital Identity or SPID enables Italian citizens and residents to access all government services provided by the Public Administration by using one Digital Identity that comprises a username and password.

19. In Italy, the Police Headquarters, or Police Central Office, is called *"Questura."*

20. A *"Nulla Osta"* can be a Work Permit, a Certification, an Authorization, an Entry Clearance, or a Waiver.

21. The Lira.

22. Italian citizens are typically automatically assigned a Tax Identification Number at birth, a unique 16-character code, including letters and numbers

based on your personal information, such as your name, date of birth, and place of birth.

23. Healthcare in Italy is primarily provided through a universal public healthcare system known as the National Health Service or SSN, "*Servizio Sanitario Nazionale*," which gives all Italian citizens and legal residents access to comprehensive and accessible healthcare services, regardless of their financial status.

24. Buying property in Italy might help getting a visa since it gives you an address in Italy but it doesn't qualify for getting a visa.

25. There are 20 administrative regions in Italy, Abruzzo, Basilicata, Calabria, Campania, Emilia-Romagna, Friuli-Venezia Giulia, Lazio, Liguria, Lombardy, Marche, Molise, Piedmont, Apulia (Puglia), Sardinia (Sardegna), Sicily (Sicilia), Tuscany (Toscana), Trentino-Alto Adige (Trentino-South Tyrol), Umbria, Aosta Valley (Valle d'Aosta) and Veneto.

26. It will take a boat ride or a flight to get off the islands.

27. Southern Italy.

28. Besides the prestige, buying property in Italy is a great investment, especially if it is in a big city or a region with lots of expats.

Faraglioni by night, Capri, Italy

VOCABULARY / LEXIQUE

VOCABOLARIO/ LESSICO

- ATMs (Automated Teller Machines) "*Bancomat*"
- Automatic Billing / Payments "*Addebito Diretto*"
- Certificate of Incorporation "*Atto Costitutivo*" or "*Atto di Costituzione*"
- Certificate of No Impediment "*Nulla Osta*"
- Checking Accounts "*Conto Corrente*"
- Citizenship through ancestry "*Jus Sanguinis*"
- Dog Registry "*Anagrafe Canina*"
- Employment Office "*Ufficio Provinciale del Lavoro e della Massima Occupazione*"
- Elective Residency Visa "*Residenza Elettiva*"
- Family Doctors "*Medici di Base*"
- Fingerprints "*Cattura degli impronte digitali*"
- Flow Decree "*Decreto Flussi*"
- Foreign Department "Ufficio Stranieri"
- High Speed Train "*Treno Alta Velocità*"
- Immigration Office "*Sportello Unico per l'Immigrazione*"

VOCABULARY / LEXIQUE | VOCABOLARIO/ LESSICO

☞ Investor Visa "*Visto Per Investitori*"
☞ Italian Chamber of Commerce "*Camera di Commercio*"
☞ Italian Revenue Agency "*Agenzia delle Entrate*"
☞ Limited Liability Company (LLC) "*Società a Responsabilità Limitata*" (SRL)
☞ Municipal Tax "*Tassa sui Servizi Indivisibili*"
☞ National Business Register "*Registro delle Imprese*"
☞ National Health Service "*Servizio Sanitario Nazionale*" (SSN)
☞ National Revenue Agency "*Agenzia delle Entrate*"
☞ Night or on-duty pharmacy "*Farmacia di Turno*"
☞ Night or on-call doctor "*Medico di Guardia*" or "*Medico Notturno*"
☞ Non-profits Organisations "*Patronati*"
☞ Police Department "*Questura*"
☞ Post Office "*Poste*"
☞ Property Tax "*Imposta Municipale Propria*"
☞ Residence Permit "*Permesso di Soggiorno*"
☞ Residence Permit for Start-up Entrepreneurs "*Permesso di Soggiorno per Intraprendenti*"
☞ Registry Office "*Anagrafe*"
☞ Restricted Driving Areas "*Zona Traffico Limitato*" (ZTL)

- Savings account "*Conto Risparmio*"
- Scattered or dispersed hotels "*Alberghi Diffusi*"
- Security deposit "*Cauzione*"
- Social Security System "*Sistema di Sicurezza Sociale*"
- Tax Identification Number "*Codice Fiscale*"
- Tax Office "*Agenzia delle Entrate*"
- Tax Registrar (*Registro delle Imposte*)
- Town Hall, City Hall, Municipality "*Comune*"
- Value Added Tax "*Imposta sul Valore Aggiunto*"
- Vehicle Registration Office "*Pubblico Registro Automobilistico*"
- Wealth Tax "*Imposta sulle Grandi Fortune*"
- Work Visa for Self-Employed Individuals "*Lavoro Autonomo*"

REFERENCES
BIBLIOGRAPHIA

Italian Embassies: The embassies' websites have sections on visas and residency requirements, as well as information on studying, working, Italian laws for pets, and doing business in Italy.

The Ministry of Foreign Affairs and International Cooperation's website has a special section for foreigners moving to Italy (visas, permits, and citizenship)

The Italian National Tourist Board has information regarding residency, healthcare, and Culture

InterNations is a Social Network for ex-pats and practical aspects of living in Italy

The official website of the Italian Customs Authority (Agenzia delle Dogane e dei Monopoli) provides information on import regulations, customs procedures, and required documentation. Visit their website at *www.agenziadoganemonopoli.gov.it*.

To learn more about visas, housing, and healthcare, go to Expat.com/Italy

To learn more Italian:
https://www.myitalianlessons.co.uk/singular-to-plural-in-italian/ Or *https://www.mosalingua.com/en/10-essential-italian-slang-expressions/*

To learn more about the types of visas and duration, go to: *https://www.esteri.it/en/servizi-consolari-e-visti/ingressosoggiornoinitalia/visto_ingresso/tipologie_visto_durata/*

To learn more about ETIAS, go to:
https://www.handyvisas.com/visa-policy/italy/

To learn more about self-employed visas, go to:
https://visaguide.world/europe/italy-visa/long-stay/self-employment/

To learn more about the EU Blue card,
https://visaguide.world/europe/eu-blue-card/italy/

To learn more about Italy's investor visa, visit
https://investorvisa.mise.gov.it

Italy Digital Nomads - 12 Most Popular Places to Stay & Work. *https://nomadgirl.co/italy-digital-nomads-12-most-popular-places-to-stay-work/*

Italian Citizenship: *https://www.thinkinitalian.com/how-to-obtain-italian-citizenship-a-comprehensive-guide/*

To learn more about the Italy Digital Visa, go to:
https://esim.holafly.com/travel-tips/digital-nomad-visa-italy/ https://heymondo.com/blog/italy-digital-nomad-visa/ https://arlettipartners.com/digital-nomad-visa-italy/

To learn more about Start-up visas, go to
https://italiastartupvisa.mise.gov.it/#Why_Italy.

If you are looking for a hotel in Italy, go to:
https://www.meininger-hotels.com/blog/en/category/destinations/italy/

"There is no place like Italy" https://americadomani.com

European Luxury Property. https://europeanproperty.com

If you are wondering where the best towns for nomads are, https://travelingrauf.com/best-digital-nomad-places-in-italy/

To learn more about Sicily, visitsicily.com

To learn more about life in Rome, https://www.expatslivinginrome.com

If you want to learn more about Genoa, https://lionsinthepiazza.com/genoa-day/

To find a list of cities for digital nomads, https://nomadlist.com

This Facebook group will help you find lodging anywhere in Italy:
https://www.facebook.com/groups/255069514022102/

https://beelinguapp.com/blog/amore-and-other-charming-italian-terms-of-endearment

To learn more about Startup Visa: https://www.ttn-taxation.net/pdfs/Speeches_NewYork_2018/8.AlessandraPagani-HowtoobtainastartupvisainItaly.pdf

To learn more about the One Euro Housing Program, go to *https://1eurohouses.com/1-euro-houses-map/*

To find out if you need a visa to Italy, go to *https://vistoperitalia.esteri.it/home/en*

To rent a home in Italy, visit Vrbo: *https://www.vrbo.com/vacation-rentals/europe/italy*.

If you don't know which VPN to use based on location, go to *https://findervpn.com.*

www.ingramcontent.com/pod-product-compliance
Lightning Source LLC
Chambersburg PA
CBHW051620010526
44119CB00009B/213